Finger Lakes Wineries

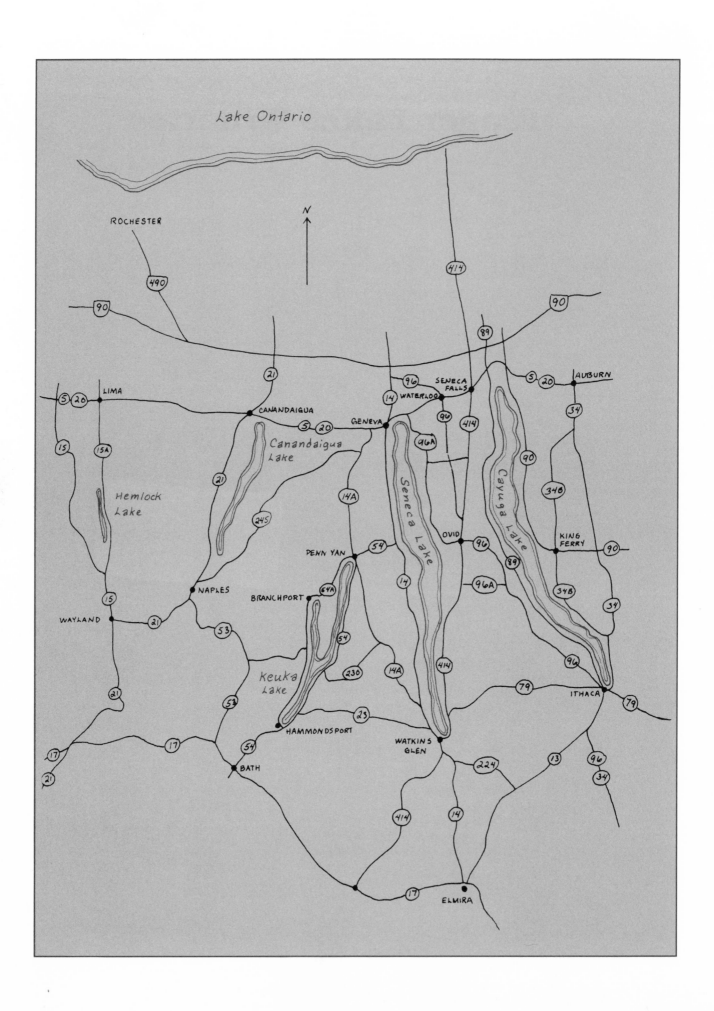

Finger Lakes Wineries

second edition

A COMPLETE TOURING GUIDE

TO CENTRAL NEW YORK'S

ACCLAIMED WINE COUNTRY

by Susan Wiener

McBooks Press • Ithaca, New York

Book and cover design by Mary A. Scott
Photographs by Susan Wiener
Cover art by Mary Shelley, 109 Park Place, Ithaca, NY 14850

Library of Congress Cataloging-in-Publication Data

Wiener, Susan, 1957-
   Finger Lakes wineries : a complete touring guide to central New
York's acclaimed wine country, second edition / by Susan Wiener
     p. cm.
   Includes index
   ISBN 0-935526-19-6 (pbk.) : $12.95
   1. Wineries–New York (State)–Finger Lakes Region–Guide-books.
2. Finger Lakes Region (N.Y.)–Description and travel–Guide-books.
I. Title.
TP557.W685 1992
641.2'2'0257478–dc20   90-6200
                                   CIP

ISBN 0-935526-19-6

This book is distributed to the book trade by several several
wholesalers and by McBooks Press, 908 Steam Mill Road,
Ithaca, NY 14850. Please write for the most recent McBooks
Press catalog. Individuals may order this books through
bookstores or directly from McBooks Press. Please include
$1.50 postage and handling with mail orders.

Printed in the United States of America
Second edition 1992

TABLE OF CONTENTS

> Grapes grown are listed in alphabetical order.
> Wines produced are listed in the order in which one would taste them: champagnes first, then white wines from driest to sweetest, then blush or rosé wines, then red wines, and finally dessert wines.

KEY

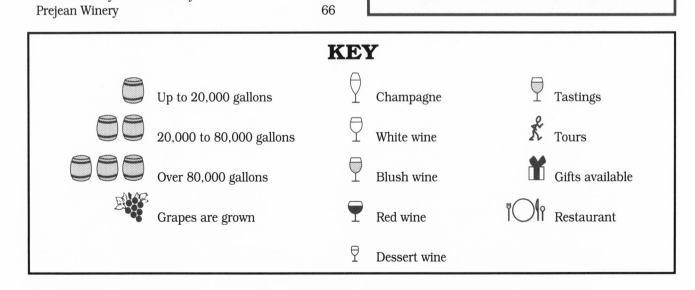

- Up to 20,000 gallons
- 20,000 to 80,000 gallons
- Over 80,000 gallons
- Grapes are grown
- Champagne
- White wine
- Blush wine
- Red wine
- Dessert wine
- Tastings
- Tours
- Gifts available
- Restaurant

INTRODUCTION

As an international wine tourist, I discovered the Finger Lakes region in 1987. I enjoyed the openness and eagerness of the winery owners and winemakers. They share an excitement about the area's potential as an internationally acclaimed wine region. I've enjoyed my winery experiences here so much that I've attempted to assist others to tour the region with this guide. This book offers in one document an up-to-date, easy-to-use informational guide to the Finger Lakes wineries.

The book includes a short history of grape growing and winemaking in the Finger Lakes and contains brief explanations of winemaking and wine tasting. All operational wineries opened through June 1992 are included. The wineries are listed by lake and then are arranged in a clockwise tour starting at the southern tip. Each winery entry includes specific data about the winery, as well as general information of interest about what makes that winery special (and they all are). Each entry also includes a detailed map, and an accurate map of the whole area at the front of the book will help you plan your trip throughout this wine region. This is a lovely area to get lost in, but we hope this book will allow you to choose whether or not to be lost. The alphabetical index lists the wineries for easy reference.

Cayuga, Seneca, and Keuka Lake wineries have formed Wine Trail associations and, in conjunction with the state-funded New York Wine & Grape Foundation, have printed brochures and placed very helpful directional signs along the roads.

I would like to take this space to thank my friends and family for their help and support, and Alex Skutt for taking on and continuing with this project. Mostly, I'd like to thank the winery owners, winemakers, and grape growers for their vision, perseverance, and willingness to commit their resources and time to this risky and demanding business.

Winery visitors are encouraged to tour with a designated driver; the wineries offer grape juice for designated drivers and children. The terrain here is often quite rugged, with steep hills and sharply curved roads. Many of these are country roads, and some are not paved. Please drive safely.

Happy trails.

CANANDAIGUA LAKE, WESTERN AND NORTHERN WINERIES

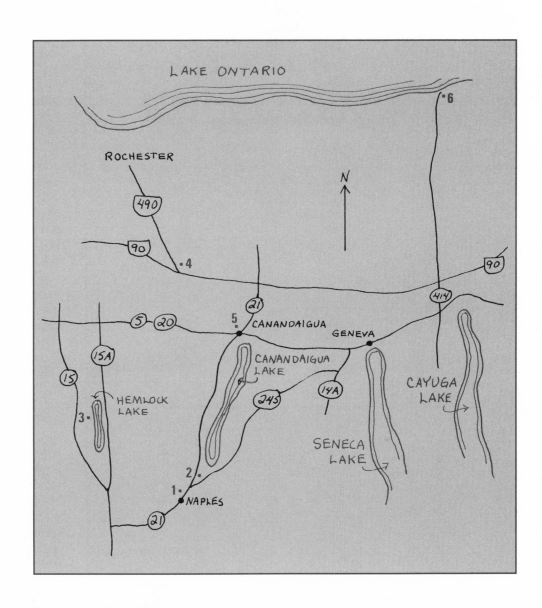

WIDMER'S WINE CELLARS

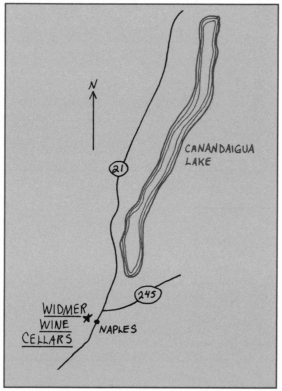

Founded in 1888 by John Jacob Widmer of Switzerland, Widmer's Wine Cellars enjoyed immediate popularity. A large winery in its own right, Widmer was recently purchased by the huge Canandaigua Wine Company. This modern winery continues many of the practices introduced by John Jacob Widmer, including the age-old Spanish method of making sherry. In this tradition, barrels of sherry are aged on the roof where they are sunbaked in summer and chilled in winter.

The popularity of Widmer's Lake Niagara wine has allowed the company to start experimenting with new wines. They've recently developed their Special Reserve Cellars, a series of fine table wines. These award-winning, drier wines feature vinifera and hybrid grapes. The company has also expanded its line of wine coolers.

Overlooking Canandaigua Lake, the winery is a huge complex of buildings. The thorough tour takes you through the cellars and bottling operation, ending with a sit-down tasting in the chalet. If visitors wish to forgo the tour and formal tasting, a twelve-minute video on the winery is shown. Widmer's Wine Shop allows one to sample wines before purchase, and the gift shop carries regional crafts, jellies and juice, tee shirts and books. Antique wine-making equipment displayed in the winery's museum makes an interesting contrast with the technology used at Widmer today.

WIDMER'S WINE CELLARS

1 Lake Niagara Lane, Naples, NY 14512
Phone: (716) 374-6311

OWNER: Canandaigua Wine Company

WINEMAKERS: Glenn Curtis, Head Winemaker
Bonnie Abrams, Special Reserve Cellars Winemaker

ESTABLISHED: Property purchased 1883
First planting 1888
First vintage 1888

PRODUCTION:

300 acres planted
300 acres in production
Over 1,000,000 gallon yield
Majority of grapes are purchased.

GRAPES GROWN:

Aurore
Baco Noir
Catawba
Cayuga White
Marechal Foch
Niagara
Rosette
Rougeon
Seyval
Vidal

WINES PRODUCED:

Widmer Extra Dry Champagne–*a blend of Cayuga and Aurore*
Crackling Lake Niagara–*a sparkling wine of Niagara, Elvira, and Moores Diamond*
Vintage Chardonnay
Chablis Blanc–*a blend of Aurore, Cayuga, and Seyval*
Rhine–*a blend of Aurore, Dutchess, and Muscat of Alexandria*
Vintage Johannisberg Riesling
Vintage Seyval Blanc
Lake Niagara Light–*a blend of Niagara and Elvira*
Lake Niagara–*a blend of Niagara, Elvira, and Moores Diamond*
Sauterne–*made from Delaware*
Haut Sauterne–*made from Delaware*
Blush Chablis–*a blend of Seyval and Cayuga*
Lake Niagara Blush–*a blend of Niagara and Elvira*
Vintage Cabernet Sauvignon
Burgundy–*a blend of Marechal Foch, DeChaunac, and Rougeon*
Lake Niagara Harvest Red–*a blend of Niagara and Vincent*
Pale Dry Sherry–*a blend of Concord and Elvira*
Sherry–*a blend of Concord and Elvira*
Cream Sherry–*a blend of Concord and Elvira*
Special Selection Cream Sherry–*a blend of Concord and Elvira*
Port–*a blend of Marechal Foch, Chelois, DeChaunac, and Concord*
Lake Niagara Wine Cooler
Lake Niagara Blush Cooler–*blending Niagara and Vincent*
Lake Niagara Harvest Red Cooler–*blending Niagara and Vincent*
Harvest Hill Peach Cooler
Harvest Hill Strawberry Cooler

RECENT AWARDS: Numerous awards received, including:
NV Lake Niagara–*1991 New York Wine & Food Classic, Silver Medal; 1991 International Eastern Wine Competition, Silver Medal; 1991 Tasters Guild, Silver Medal; 1991 Florida State Fair, Bronze Medal*
NV Crackling Lake Niagara–*1991 New York State Fair, Silver Medal*
NV Extra Dry Champagne–*1991 TG, Bronze Medal*
NV Cream Sherry–*1991 IEWC, Silver Medal; 1991 TG, Silver Medal; 1991 Intervin, Bronze Medal*
NV Port–*1991 TG, Bronze Medal*
1989 Dry Riesling–*1991 San Diego Wine Competition, Silver Medal; 1991 NYW&FC, Silver Medal; 1991 NYSF, Silver Medal; 1991 International Wine & Spirits Competition, Bronze Medal*
1988 Cabernet Sauvignon–*1991 NYSF, Silver Medal; 1991 NYW&FC, Bronze Medal; 1991 IW&SC, Bronze Medal*

PRICING: $2.49 to $12.99 per bottle; discounts available.
MasterCard, Visa and American Express accepted.

AVAILABILITY: Available throughout the northeastern US and in some southern states.

TASTINGS AND TOURS:

Open June through October, Monday through Saturday, 10 AM to 4 PM; Sunday, 11:30 AM to 4:30 PM.
Open November through May, daily, 1 PM to 4 PM.
Closed Thanksgiving, Christmas, New Year's Day, and Easter.
No charge for tastings. Wine tastings available in the wine shop; tastings of gourmet jellies and juices available in the gift shop.
Tours are available.

Noir

11% Alcohol by Volume 750ml.

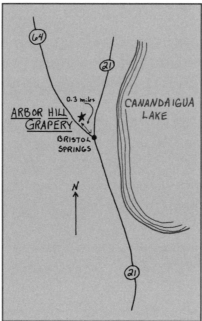

John Brahms is no stranger to the wine industry. After earning a degree in agriculture, he worked with Widmer's Wine Cellars for twenty-three years, retiring in 1987. Since 1971, he and his brother have been growing grapes and providing juice to home winemakers. John himself started making wines to allow his home-winemaking customers to taste a finished wine from each grape variety.

Today, John and his wife Katie have their own winery, where many of their wines are graced with unique labels depicting the lake boats of old. Located right in the small town of Bristol Springs, the Brahms have two shops side by side. In one, wine tastings are offered, cheeses are tasted and sold, and wine accessories are available for purchase. The other shop stocks the Brahms' extensive line of wine sauces and jellies, as well as gift baskets, gourmet specialty foods, and country gifts. A warm, old-fashioned atmosphere exudes from both Victorian-style shops.

On very busy weekends, tastings overflow into the barn or tents set up behind the shops. At these times, besides their year round offering of grape pies, kuchen, and danish, visitors can enjoy hot grape sundaes and wine sausage. The Brahms maintain a mail order catalog and their gift baskets are very popular. Their food products are available in gift shops throughout the state.

It is a beautiful scenic drive to Arbor Hill Grapery, located near Naples, overlooking Canandaigua Lake. With the Ontario County Park just across the street, a visit to this winery can be part of a fine day's outing.

ARBOR HILL GRAPERY

6459 Route 64, Naples, NY 14512
Phone: (716) 374-2870

OWNERS: John and Katie Brahms

WINEMAKER: John Brahms

ESTABLISHED:
Property purchased 1964
First planting 1971
First vintage 1987

PRODUCTION:
17 acres planted
17 acres in production
3,000 gallon yield
Some grapes are purchased; grapes and juice are sold.

GRAPES GROWN:

Aurore	Delaware	Vidal
Catawba	Marechal Foch	Vignoles
Cayuga	Niagara	Vincent
Concord	Seyval	
DeChaunac	Sheridan	

WINES PRODUCED:

Arbor Hill label:
Arbor Hill Celebration–*a sparkling wine blended from Vidal, Cayuga, and Gewurztraminer*
Chardonnay
Riesling
Moores Diamond
Arbor Hill Noir–*made from Marechal Foch*
Lake Boat label:
Lady of the Lake–*Chardonnay in half-bottles*
Vignoles
Onnalinda White–*a blend of Vidal, Riesling, and Gewurztraminer*
Lake Boat Niagara
Lake Boat Blush–*a blend of Cayuga and Sheridan*

RECENT AWARDS:
1989 Chardonnay–*1991 New York Wine & Food Classic, Bronze Medal; 1990 International Eastern Wine Competition, Bronze Medal*
1989 Arbor Hill Noir–*1991 NYW&FC, Silver Medal*
1989 Celebration–*1990 IEWC, Bronze Medal*
NV Ogarita-Niagara–*1991 NYW&FC, Bronze Medal*
NV Genundewah-Blush–*1991 NYW&FC, Bronze Medal*

PRICING:
$3.50 to $8.95 per bottle; case discounts available.
MasterCard and Visa accepted.

AVAILABILITY:
At local liquor stores and restaurants.
Food products available in gift shops throughout New York State

TASTINGS AND TOURS:
Open Memorial Day Weekend through Christmas, Monday through Saturday, 10 AM to 5 PM; Sunday, noon to 5 PM.
Open January through May, Saturday 10 AM to 5 PM; Sunday, noon to 5PM or by appointment.
No charge for tastings of both wines and cheeses.
Tours not available.

EAGLE CREST VINEYARDS

O·NEH·DA®

ESTABLISHED 1872   CONTAINS SULFITES

ALTAR WINE
100% *Pure Grape Wine*
New York State

ST. MICHAEL'S RED

Full Bodied and Ruby Red, This Wine is Sweet and Fruity
ALCOHOL 11.5% BY VOLUME

Cellared and bottled by O-Neh-Da Vineyard Conesus, NY 14435
BW-NY-686 Winery Established by Most Rev. Bernard J. McQuaid D.D.
First Bishop of Rochester Diocese, New York.

The Old Mission

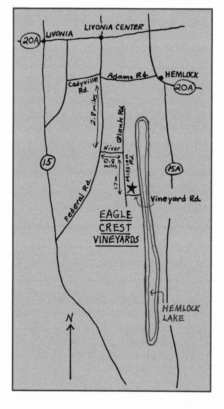

Eagle Crest Vineyards produces wine under three labels. The oldest label, O-Neh-Da, has been on sacramental wine since the late 1800's. These wines are not available for retail sale, although those who have taken communion may well have tasted one of these altar wines sold in thirty states.

The Barry label joined the O-Neh-Da company in 1968, and, in 1982, present owner Michael Secretan purchased the two labels, adding the new name, Eagle Crest. The altar wines retain the O-Neh-Da label, table wines previously released under the Barry label retain that name, and any new wines bear the Eagle Crest label.

To produce sacramental wines, an approbation license is required. The wines must be 100% grape product, with no water or sugar added. Even with these limitations, winemaker Robert Beckmann strives for a consistent taste year to year since church officials do not seek vintage variety and instead prefer the taste of the sacramental wines to remain consistent.

The entire winery exudes an aura of antiquity. In the lower cellar, no longer used, a college group once filmed an Edgar Allen Poe story. The main cellar is filled with large oak casks, some over 100 years old. The ground floor holds oak casks which hold over 5,000 gallons each.

A beautiful drive through the countryside leads to Eagle Crest Vineyards. Built in the nineteenth century on the western shore of Hemlock Lake, the winery is so far off the beaten track that it now offers tours and tastings to groups only by appointment. However, the winery is open year round for retail sales, and has a small outdoor pavilion with picnic tables.

EAGLE CREST VINEYARDS

7107 Vineyard Road, Conesus, NY 14435
Phone: (716) 346-2321

OWNER: Michael Secretan

WINEMAKER: Robert Beckmann

ESTABLISHED:
Property purchased 1982
First planting 1963
First vintage 1872

PRODUCTION:
8 acres planted
8 acres in production
30,000 gallon yield
Most grapes are purchased.

GRAPES GROWN: Niagara

WINES PRODUCED:
O-Neh-Da label:
Eleven varieties of sacramental wine
Barry label:
Chablis—*a blend of Cayuga, Vidal, Vignoles, and Seyval*
Niagara
Pink Delaware
Rose—*a blend of Cayuga, Seyval, Vidal and Chancellor*
Mellow Burgundy—*100% Chancellor*
Cream Sherry

RECENT AWARDS: Do not enter competitions.

PRICING: $3.25 per bottle, with Cream Sherry $5.75; discounts available.
Credit cards not accepted.

AVAILABILITY: Available in liquor stores locally.

TASTINGS AND TOURS: Open year round for retail sales, Monday through Friday, 9 AM to 4:30 PM.
Tastings and tours for groups only, by appointment.

CASA LARGA VINEYARDS

Originally from Italy, Andrew Colaruotolo is today a successful builder in the Rochester area. Andrew retained some acreage from land acquired for a housing development and, drawing on experience with his family's vineyards in Italy, established Casa Larga Vineyards. One of the few Finger Lakes wineries not directly on a lake, Casa Larga's altitude and slope provide fine growing conditions, according to John Colaruotolo, Andrew's son and vineyard manager. The location also offers a unique view of the Rochester skyline rising over the vineyards.

The Colaruotolos first planted native and hybrid varieties in 1974, thinking that was all that could be grown here. Upon meeting Dr. Frank, the first person to success-fully grow vinifera grapes in the Finger Lakes, the Colaruotolos ripped out most of their original plantings and planted vinifera. Today, they farm 90% vinifera grapes.

This winery has one of the most extensive physical facilities of the farm wineries. The recently built Vintage Room, along with the Tirage Room, can accommodate 450 people for weddings and corporate con-

ferences. Craft shows and other activities are often held here. They recently added 7000 square feet to process the maturing grapes resulting from their recent vineyard expansion. Additional red wine grapes will be planted, and the winemaking facilities will again be expanded as they mature. However, Casa Larga's next expansion target is the tasting room. Presently, tastings in this Italianate room, with a long tasting bar and small gift display, overflow into the oak ageing cellar.

Casa Larga uses only Yugoslavian oak, which is made into barrels in Italy. They believe this oak imparts a lighter flavor, allowing more fruit to come through, creating sophisticated wines unmasked by heavy oak. The Colaruotolos strongly believe that wine should go with food and food should go with wine. They produce only dry table wines with an alcohol content no higher than 11½%.

This modern winery has a large deck and picnic tables outside. At Casa Larga's annual Pre-Harvest Gala Festival in September, their Vidal Blanc is released with a label designed by a local artist. For a small fee, the winery will print personalized labels.

Casa Larga

Vineyard Hill
Chardonnay
Finger Lakes

Alcohol 11.5% by volume.

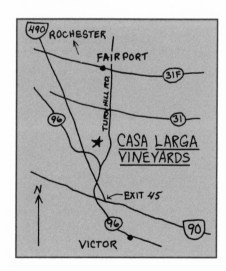

CASA LARGA VINEYARDS

Mailing address: 27 Emerald Hill Circle, Fairport, NY 14450
Winery address: 2287 Turk Hill Road, Fairport, NY 14450
Phone: (716) 223-4210

OWNERS: Andrew and Ann Colaruotolo

WINEMAKER: Andrew Colaruotolo

ESTABLISHED: Property purchased early 1960's
First plantings 1974 and 1975
First vintage 1978

PRODUCTION: 35 acres planted
27 acres in production
25,000 gallon yield
Grapes are neither purchased nor sold.

GRAPES GROWN:

Aurore	Delaware	Pinot Blanc
Cabernet Sauvignon	Gewurztraminer	Pinot Noir
Chardonnay	Merlot	Riesling
DeChaunac	Muscat Ottonel	Vidal

WINES PRODUCED:

Blanc de Blanc Naturel–*a very dry sparkling wine made from Chardonnay*
Blanc de Blanc Brut–*a sparkling wine made from Chardonnay*
Brut d'Ottonel–*a sparkling wine made from Muscat Ottonel*
Chardonnay
Vineyard Hill Chardonnay
Johannisberg Riesling
Gewurztraminer
Pinot Blanc

Vidal Blanc
Estate White–*a blend of Vidal and Aurore*
Estate Blush–*a blend of Vidal, Aurore, and DeChaunac*
Estate Rosé–*100% DeChaunac*
Petite Noir–*100% DeChaunac*
Estate Red–*a blend of DeChaunac, Chelois, and Rougeon*
Pinot Noir
Cabernet Sauvignon

RECENT AWARDS:
NV Brut d'Ottonel–*1991 International Eastern Wine Competition, Bronze Medal*
1990 Estate Red–*1991 New York State Fair, Gold Medal*
1989 Johannisberg Riesling–*1991 NYSF, Gold Medal*
1989 Vidal Blanc–*1991 NYSF, Bronze Medal*
1989 Petite Noir–*1991 NYSF, Bronze Medal*
1988 Chardonnay–*1991 Dallas Morning News Wine Competition, Bronze Medal*
1987 Cabernet Sauvignon–*1991 New York Wine & Food Classic, Gold Medal*

PRICING: $4.99 to $15.00 per bottle; discounts available.
MasterCard, Visa, American Express, and Discover Card accepted.

AVAILABILITY: At restaurants and liquor stores in the Rochester area.

TASTINGS AND TOURS: Open all year, Monday through Saturday, 10 AM to 6 PM; Sunday, noon to 6 PM; closed New Year's Day, Easter, Thanksgiving, and Christmas.
No charge for tastings.
Guided tours available all year.

CANANDAIGUA WINE COMPANY

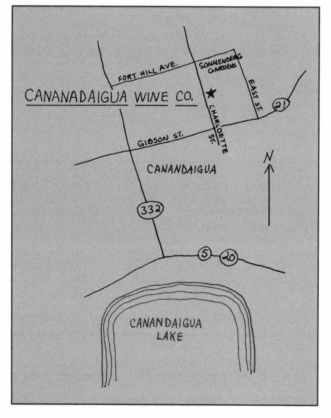

Established in 1946, Canandaigua Wine Company is now the third largest winery in the United States. With a capacity measured in the millions of gallons, the company is in a different league from the small farm wineries which populate the Finger Lakes. Canandaigua Wine Company is continually growing and currently owns eleven wine companies producing hundreds of brands, as well as a wine import business. Widmer's Wine Cellars, purchased by Canandaigua Wine Company in 1986, continues to offer its own tastings, tours, and shops at its Naples, New York location.

A growth-oriented company focusing on long term development, Canandaigua Wine Company seeks to offer the best wine at the best price. They work to make wines that meet the public's desires and, in their quest for quality, seek to avoid cutting corners.

Many of Canandaigua Wine Company's products are available for tasting and purchase at the former country home of Frederick and Mary Clark Thompson, Sonnenberg Gardens, in Canandaigua, New York. The fifty-acre estate, with its large mansion and many formal gardens, may be explored on one's own or on a guided tour. The lovely tasting room, once a canning cellar, features stained-glass windows and a fountain. A popular attraction, it can become quite crowded on holiday weekends.

CANANDAIGUA WINE COMPANY

Business address: 116 Buffalo Street, Canandaigua, NY 14424
Phone: (716) 394-7900
Tasting room: 151 Charlotte Street, Canandaigua, NY 14424
Phone: (716) 394-7680

OWNER: Canandaigua Wine Company

WINEMAKER: Dominic Carisetti

ESTABLISHED: Property purchased 1946
First vintage 1946

PRODUCTION: Third largest wine producer in the United States
All grapes are purchased, except at Widmer's Wine Cellars.

WINES PRODUCED: **Wines produced under numerous labels, including:**

Batavia Wine Cellars	Skye's Hollow
Chase-Limogere Champagne	Sun Country Wine Coolers
Cisco	Widmer's Wine Cellars
Cooks Champagne	Wild Irish Rose
Cooks Varietals	
Cribari	**Wines imported:**
Dunnewood	Keller Geister
Italian Swiss Colony	Marcus James
J. Roget Champagne	Mateus
Manischewitz Wines	Mondoro

RECENT AWARDS: Numerous awards received, including:
NV American Vino Casata Blush Chablis–*1991 Les Amis du Vin, Gold Medal*
NV J. Roget Asti Spumante–*1991 Dallas Morning News Wine Competition, Silver Medal; 1991 San Francisco Fair, Bronze Medal*
NV Mateus White–*1991 Tasters Guild, Bronze Medal*
NV Mondoro Asti Spumanti–*1991 DMNWC, Gold Medal; 1991 International Wine & Spirits Competition, Silver Medal*
NV Skye's Hollow White–*1991 International Eastern Wine Competition, Silver Medal*
NV Skye's Hollow Strawberry–*1991 DMNWC, Bronze Medal*
1989 Manischewitz Chardonnay–*1991 LADV, Silver Medal*
1990 Marcus James White Zinfandel–*1991 IW&SC, Bronze Medal*
1989 Marcus James Chardonnay–*1991 Florida State Fair, Silver Medal; 1991 W&SC, Bronze Medal*
1988 Marcus James Cabernet Sauvignon–*1991 IW&SC, Silver Medal*
Widmer's Wine Cellars awards listed on page 11.

PRICING: $3.29 to $12.99 per bottle; discounts available.
MasterCard and Visa accepted.

AVAILABILITY: Throughout the US.

TASTINGS AND TOURS: Open June through August, daily, noon to 4 PM.
Open May, September, and October, Saturday and Sunday, noon to 4 PM.
No charge for tastings.
Tours are not available.

Chimney Heights

Pinot Noir

New York State
Produced and Bottled By
Thorpe Vineyard

East Bay, Wolcott, NY

ALCOHOL 11% BY VOLUME   CONTAINS SULFITES

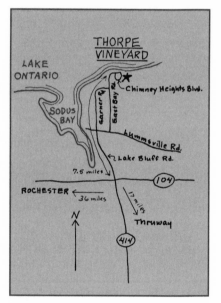

Bob Straubing started Straubing Vineyard in the 1980's. When he began spending half the year in Florida, he couldn't attend the grapes properly, so he decided to sell the property.

Enter Jock and Fumie Thorpe. He's from the area and works in construction, she's from Japan and came here to study at a local university. They found this property and decided to take on the challenge of running a small winery. Bob Straubing and his friend, an amateur winemaker, walked them through the first harvest. Fumie now runs the winery, with Jock providing moral support. They both attend events at the Agricultural Experimental Station and visit other wineries.

Starting with the single acre previously planted, they've added three more acres but don't expect to exceed a total of five acres of grapes. They consider Thorpe Vineyard perhaps the nation's smallest winery, currently producing 500 gallons of wine annually, and don't plan to produce more than 2400 gallons per year. The winery shares a small red and white pole barn with equipment and an office/tasting room.

Thorpe Vineyard is actually outside of the Finger Lakes appellation, but is included here because it's closest to this region. Located right on Lake Ontario, the winery is open for tastings on weekends in season. Thorpe Vineyard wines bear the name Chimney Heights. Their Chardonnay and Cayuga White are each available in standard or 1.5 liter bottles.

THORPE VINEYARD

8150 Chimney Heights Boulevard., Wolcott, NY 14590
Phone: (315) 594-2502

OWNER: Fumie Thorpe

WINEMAKER: Fumie Thorpe

ESTABLISHED:
Property purchased 1988
First planting 1978
First vintage 1988

PRODUCTION:

4 acres planted
1 acre in production
500 gallon yield
Some grapes are purchased

GRAPES GROWN:

Cayuga White
Chardonnay
Marechal Foch
Melody
Pinot Gris
Pinot Noir
Riesling

WINES PRODUCED:

Chimney Heights label:
Chardonnay
Cayuga White
Estate Blanc—*a blend of Cayuga and Riesling*
Pinot Noir

RECENT AWARDS: Have yet to enter competitions.

PRICING: $5.00 to $12.00 (for 1.5 liter Chardonnay); quantity discounts available.
Credit cards are not accepted.

AVAILABILITY: Local liquor stores and restaurants.

TASTINGS AND TOURS:

Open Memorial Day through October, Saturday, Sunday, and holidays,
noon to 6 PM, and by appointment.
Open weekends before Thanksgiving and Christmas; call ahead.
No charge for tastings.

HISTORY OF GRAPE GROWING AND WINEMAKING IN THE FINGER LAKES

The Finger Lakes and the Lake Effect

The Finger Lakes, long, parallel bodies of water carved by Ice Age glaciers, frame a unique and productive grape-growing region. Although the latitude is the same as that of the major French wine regions, Finger Lakes winters are colder and harsher. However, these very deep lakes remain unfrozen, creating the "lake effect" which protects the surrounding slopes. The lakes heat the winter air, causing it to rise. Cold air then flows down the slopes to fill the space above the lake. This circulation of the air keeps the cold from blanketing the land and forming deadly pockets of frost. The lake effect has been defined in a Cornell University study as extending about one and one half miles inland and no more than 617 feet above the lake.

Early American Grape Growing

Wild grapes grew profusely through early America. Dissatisfied with wine made from these grapes, settlers attempted to plant European vinifera grapes for winemaking. American soil proved inhospitable to the young imported vines, which could not survive attack by the Phylloxera grape root aphid in spite of the determined efforts of the growers. In time the settlers found a way

out of their dilemma when they discovered in the wild new varieties of grapes more suited to their purpose. It is now believed that these grapes were the result of natural cross-pollination of wild grapes and the short-lived vinifera. Today these grapes are considered the native American grapes, and make up the labrusca family, including Concord, Isabella, and Catawba grapes.

Europe had its own problems with the grape root aphid, which found its way from the States to European vineyards in the late nineteenth century. Grape growers replanted their decimated fields with vinifera grafted onto the more resistant American rootstock. Eventually, hybrids between European and American grapes were produced with the heartiness of the American rootstock and some of the more complex characteristics of the European grapes. When introduced in the United States, these hybrids caught on in the Finger Lakes region.

The Birth and Death of the First Wineries

The first grapes planted in the Finger Lakes in the early nineteenth century were for sacramental wine. By 1860 the first commercial winery, the Hammondsport and Pleasant Valley Wine Company, was founded. Winning an award at the 1867 Paris Exposition, their Catawba sparkling wine was elsewhere proclaimed the "greatest champagne of the Western world." From this came the winery's current name "Great Western." The nineteenth century also saw the founding of Gold Seal Vineyards, Taylor Wine Company, and Widmer's Wine Cellars–as well as the Temperance Movement.

Federal Prohibition heralded the death of many American wineries. A few stayed alive by making juice, jams, jellies, sacramental wine, and juice for home winemakers. Limited home winemaking remained legal, and the number of home winemakers increased during the Prohibition years. At least one winery marketed its grape juice with very specific instructions on how not to turn the juice into wine, "do not add yeast and let ferment...." In spite of these tactics, by the time Prohibition was repealed in 1933, the wine industry was all but destroyed. However, the largest New York wineries somehow survived, and with time, more and more farmers found wine grapes a steady cash crop.

Why Vinifera?

In post-Prohibition years, wines in the Finger Lakes were made from labrusca grapes and from hybrids produced both in Europe and locally at the Geneva Agricultural Experiment Station. The European vinifera grapes still were not hardy enough to survive the Finger Lakes winters. Dr. Konstantin Frank, a Ukrainian specialist in frigid terrain vineyards, brought the expertise to successfully grow vinifera here. Fleeing the Ukraine during the second World War, his final destination was the Finger Lakes, where he settled in 1951. He had the opportunity to practice his skills when he was hired by Charles Fournier at Great Western. Having grown vinifera grapes in Russia and Bavaria, Dr. Frank recognized the need for disease-resistant rootstock which produces ripe grapes within the given growing season. His experiments led him to graft vinifera vine cuttings onto Canadian rootstock with a one hundred day growing season, producing the first healthy vinifera grapes on the east coast.

Vinifera did not immediately catch on in the Finger Lakes. Dr. Frank

started his own vineyards, but he was more interested in experimenting than in marketing. While California wines were sweeping the country, New York State continued to be a conservative farming area. It wasn't until farm wineries sprang up, selling limited amounts of quality wine, that vinifera grapes gained a stronger toehold.

The Farm Winery Act

The New York State Farm Winery Act of 1976 changed the face of the state's wine industry. Wineries had been required to sell 95% of their wines through distributors; the Act now permitted wineries of a limited size to sell their wines directly to consumers. This encourages the establishment of small wineries with production too limited to be carried

by a distributor, and wineries may now receive the full retail price for their work.

The passage of the Farm Winery Act came by chance at an opportune time for the many grape growers affected by the 1977 purchase of Taylor Wine Company by the Coca Cola Company. Many growers had for years sold exclusively to Taylor, but Coca Cola found California

grape prices lower, and the bottom fell out of the New York grape market. While many growers went bankrupt, others were enabled by the Farm Winery Act to open their own wineries, selling their wines directly to visitors. Many winery owners enjoy this opportunity to meet the people who purchase and enjoy their wine.

The Future

The grape and wine markets rise and fall, depending on the weather, international competition, the political climate, and the state of the economy. However, as more and more Americans appreciate a fine table wine to accompany a meal, wineries are opening in such states as Illinois and Texas, and the Finger Lakes wineries are expanding. At this time, there are forty-five Finger Lakes wineries, six of which opened in the past two years, and more are likely to open in the near future.

Wineries are continually broadening the repertoire of wines produced in the Finger Lakes, with more red vinifera grapes planted each year in addition to the labrusca, hybrid, and white vinifera for which the area has become known. Because this area shares important geographical characteristics with the Champagne region of France, many winemakers are concentrating on premium sparkling wines. The cool growing season in the Finger Lakes produces grapes with the fairly high acid levels required for well-balanced red wines and fine sparkling wines. As the vines mature and winemakers gain experience and knowledge, wines of increasingly high quality will be available. This area is expected by many to become an internationally renowned wine producing region.

KEUKA LAKE WINERIES

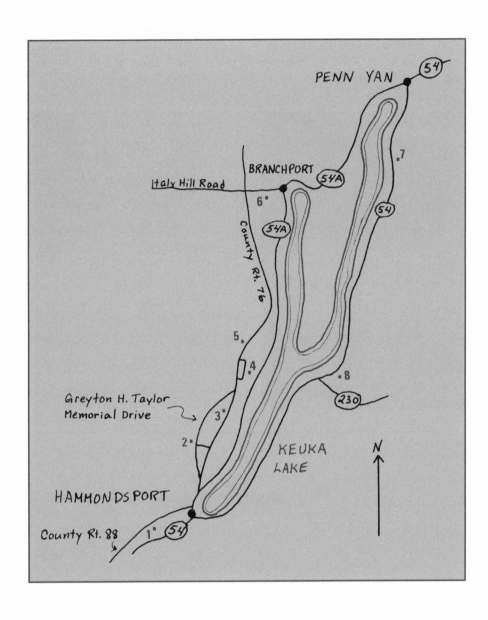

TAYLOR–GREAT WESTERN–GOLD SEAL WINERY

Taylor Wine Company, Great Western Winery, and Gold Seal Vineyards are three major New York State wineries, founded in the nineteenth century, which became large, nationally known, well-respected companies. Over time, they were each acquired by large corporations. Today Vintner's International owns all three and produces wines under the three separate labels out of a large Hammondsport plant. The old Gold Seal building along the west shore of Keuka Lake today stands empty.

The Hammondsport visitors' center is a veritable museum, with antique winemaking equipment and numerous displays. A film on each winery is shown in theaters made from 35,000-gallon redwood wine barrels, fitted with carpeted floors, seats, and movie screens. At a large wine tasting bar one may sample from among the many wines the company produces. The adjacent wine shop, the largest in the area, carries wine accessories and memorabilia.

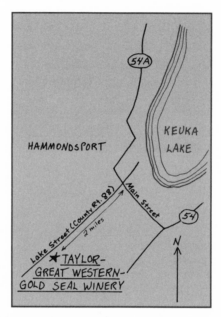

The winery complex is so large that the tour requires a bus ride. The tour includes the huge bottling operation, passes 100,000 gallon wine tanks, takes in the sherry-making operation, points out the developmental winery, and ends with a sit-down wine tasting. One visits both modern structures and century-old stone buildings, all filled with modern equipment and guided by advanced technology.

These wineries offer over seventy-five wines, ranging from champagne to dessert wines, picnic wines to older vintage wines. The developmental winery–actually a smaller winery within the large winery complex–is where new wines are developed and perfected. These include the newest line of wines, the upscale Great Western varietals, which feature hybrid and vinifera grapes. The company intends to maintain its extensive variety of wines and to continue developing new products.

TAYLOR–GREAT WESTERN–GOLD SEAL WINERY

County Route 88, Hammondsport, NY 14840
Phone: (607) 569-6111

OWNER: Vintner's International

WINEMAKERS: Steve Coon, Senior Winemaker
Bob Distler

ESTABLISHED: Taylor Wine Company founded 1880
Great Western Winery founded 1860
Gold Seal Vineyards founded 1865

PRODUCTION:

1220 acres planted
1220 acres in production
29,000,000 gallon capacity
Grapes are purchased.

GRAPES GROWN:

More than twenty-nine varieties grown, mostly French-American hybrids and labrusca.

WINES PRODUCED:

Taylor label—*thirty-three wines, including:*

blended wines	port
Lake Country wines	sherry
sparkling wines	vermouth

Great Western label—*thirty-five wines, including:*

varietal wines	port
blended wines	sherry
methode champenoise sparkling wines	vermouth

Gold Seal label—*eleven wines, including:*
blended wines
sparkling wines
Henri Marchant label—*four wines*
all sparkling wines

RECENT AWARDS: Numerous awards, including:
NV Taylor Empire Cream Sherry–*1991 New York State Fair, Silver Medal*
1989 Great Western Bunch Select Ravat–*1991 NYSF, Gold Medal*
1989 Great Western Pinot Noir–*1991 NYSF, Bronze Medal*
1988 Great Western Baco Noir–*1991 NYSF, Bronze Medal*

PRICING: $3.32 to $9.69 per bottle, with champagne up to $12.99; quantity discounts available.
MasterCard and Visa accepted.

AVAILABILITY: Available throughout the US.

TASTINGS AND TOURS:

Visitors' Center open April through December, daily, 10 AM to 4 PM.
Open January through March, Monday through Saturday, 10 AM to 4 PM.
No charge for tastings.
Guided tours frequently offered.

27

BULLY HILL VINEYARDS

Up Greyton H. Taylor Memorial Drive, high above Keuka Lake, are the winery, cafe, museum, gift shop, and bed & breakfast of Walter S. Taylor. Walter S., grandson of the Taylor Wine Company's founder Walter Taylor, left that company in 1970 in a dispute over his stand for integrity in winemaking and labelling. He went on to dedicate himself to Bully Hill Vineyards, located on the Taylor Wine Company's original site.

When the Coca Cola Company purchased Taylor Wine Company seven years later, Coca Cola sued Walter S. Taylor, demanding all rights to the Taylor name. Walter was required, by court order, to turn over to the Coca Cola Company all artwork, photographs, documents, etc., connecting the Taylor family to Bully Hill. He complied by literally dumping them on the Taylor Wine Company steps.

Since Walter can no longer use his surname in connection with Bully Hill Vineyards, his labels today are signed "Walter S. ▮▮▮▮" or "Walter S. XXXXXX." Taking this one or two steps further, he has sketched masks on portraits of Taylor family members and insists that he was raised by magical goats, the "Happy Herd." Says Walter, "They

took my name and heritage, but they didn't get my goat."

Bully Hill grows and buys primarily French-American hybrid grapes and uses them in making sixty different wines. In both taste and pricing, they are reaching out to the general public. Ingredient and blend information is scrupulously listed for all wines. As the third largest New York State winery, Bully Hill's grape purchases are a financially important support for many area growers.

A tragic car accident in 1990 left Walter a ventilator-dependent quadriplegic. With his tenacious spirit, he fought through a coma, through rehabilitation programs, and is back home. Wife Lillian and winemaker and friend Gregg Learned have continued the winery in the spirit Walter intended. New wines are to be introduced with labels Walter has recently completed using a paintbrush held in his mouth. More grapes will be planted and marketing remains strong.

A multitude of well-weathered buildings comprises the winery complex. At this very popular winery, guided tours and tastings are offered frequently. Numerous homemade signs direct visitors, and an informal and jovial atmosphere prevails throughout.

BULLY HILL® VINEYARDS

100% NEW YORK STATE
Sunny Beach Cayuga
WHITE TABLE WINE

100% Produced and Bottled by Bully Hill Vineyards, Inc.
8843 Greyton H. Taylor Memorial Drive, Hammondsport,
New York 14840 U.S.A. (607) 868-3610

OUR PRODUCTS PRODUCED BY THE WORKERS OF BULLY HILL VINEYARDS, INC. / NAMES UPON REQUEST

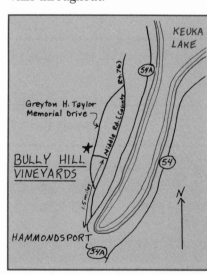

BULLY HILL VINEYARDS

8843 Greyton H. Taylor Memorial Drive, Hammondsport, NY 14840
Phone: (607) 868-3610
Fax: (607) 868-3205

OWNER: Walter S. Taylor

WINEMAKER: Gregg Learned

ESTABLISHED: Property purchased 1958
First planting 1878 by Walter S. Taylor's grandfather
First vintage 1967

PRODUCTION: 130 acres planted
120 acres in production
350,000 gallon yield
Grapes are purchased from area growers.

GRAPES GROWN: 25 varieties grown

WINES PRODUCED: Sixty wines produced, not all available at all times. A brochure at the winery has the names and exact blend information for each wine.

RECENT AWARDS: Do not enter competitions.

PRICING: $5.70 per bottle, with champagne at $14.00 and St. Walter de Bully Claret at $8.00; case discounts available.
MasterCard and Visa accepted.

AVAILABILITY: In twenty-seven states.
UPS and Air Freight delivery available.

TASTINGS AND TOURS: Open year round, Monday through Saturday, 9 AM to 5 PM; Sunday, 11 AM to 5 PM. Call for tour and tasting limitations in winter.

Closed Easter, Thanksgiving, Christmas, and New Year's Day.
Guided tours offered May through October, daily; November through April, weekends only. Call ahead to confirm.
No charge for tastings or tours.

Champagne Country Cafe open May through October, 11:30 AM to 3:30 PM daily, (607) 868-3490.
The Wine Museum of Greyton H. Taylor open daily May through October, 10 AM to 4:30 PM, (607) 868-4814.
Bully Hill Bed and Breakfast open May through October, (607) 868-3226.
Hours may vary; call ahead to confirm.

HERON HILL VINEYARDS

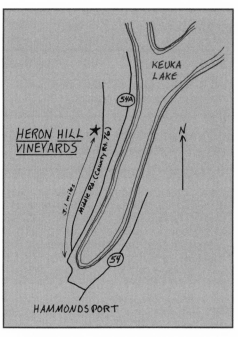

The tasting room at Heron Hill Vineyards is perched high on a hillside with a panoramic view over Keuka Lake. Large windows run the length of the tasting room and, with tables both indoors and outdoors, it is easy to get lost in the stunning scenery. At the winery, the image of the heron abounds, from the inlaid tiles of the winery's tasting room to tee shirts and locally made ceramic pitchers and bowls.

Peter Johnstone, formerly an advertising writer from New York City, fell in love with the Finger Lakes during a 1968 visit and relocated here. Co-owner John Ingle, Jr. is a grape grower on Canandaigua Lake. Peter holds that "wine is fun, and makes life a little better." He approaches winemaking with this philosophy. He specializes in white varietal wines and cultivates the individual characteristics of each. Peter strives in winemaking to achieve a high acid content balanced with the grapes' natural sugars to sustain a good, fruity characteristic in the wine.

There are no major plans for expansion at Heron Hill, although the demand for the wines has caused some increase in production. Heron Hill wines have won many awards in various competitions since 1977, and Peter Johnstone says he sees winemaking and grape growing as a fun and varied livelihood for himself and a small, almost familial staff; work from which he may never retire.

HERON HILL VINEYARDS

Middle Road, Hammondsport, NY 14840
Phone: (607) 868-4241

OWNERS: Peter Johnstone and John Ingle, Jr.

WINEMAKER: Peter Johnstone

ESTABLISHED:
Property purchased 1968
First planting 1971
First vintage 1977

PRODUCTION:

50 acres planted
50 acres in production
38,000 gallon yield
Some hybrid grapes are purchased.

GRAPES GROWN:

Chardonnay	Riesling
Muscat	Seyval
Pinot Noir	Vignoles

WINES PRODUCED:

Heron Hill label:

Chardonnay	Seyval
Riesling	Cayuga White

White Table Wine—*a blend of Aurore, Seyval, and Cayuga*
Eye of the Heron—*a blush wine blending Cayuga and Marechal Foch*
Red Table Wine—*made from Marechal Foch and Pinot Noir*
Ingle Vineyard Late Harvest Riesling

Otter Spring label:
Chardonnay
Riesling
Seyval
White Table Wine—*a blend of Vignoles, Riesling, and Cayuga*
Clairet—*a red wine made from Marechal Foch*

Little Heron label:

Chardonnay	Riesling

Simply New York's Best label:
Simply New York's Best White Table Wine—*a blend of Vignoles, Cayuga, Aurore, Seyval, and Riesling*

RECENT AWARDS:
Johannisberg Riesling—*numerous medals from 1977 to the present.*
1990 Ingle Vineyard Late Harvest Riesling—*1991 American Wine Competition, Gold Medal and Best American Sweet Riesling; 1992 San Diego National Wine Competition, Gold Medal*

PRICING:
$3.36 to $15.99 per bottle, with half-bottles of White Table Wine at $2.25; discounts available.
MasterCard, Visa, American Express, and Discover Card accepted.

AVAILABILITY: Throughout central and western New York.

TASTINGS AND TOURS:

Open May through October, Monday through Saturday, 10 AM to 5 PM; Sunday, noon to 5 PM, and by appointment.
$1.00 charge to taste three wines.
Tours available by appointment.

DR. FRANK'S VINIFERA WINE CELLARS

Dr. Konstantin Frank
1989
Rkatsiteli

NEW YORK FINGER LAKES.
ESTATE BOTTLED AND GROWN BY
KONSTANTIN D. FRANK & SONS VINIFERA WINE CELLARS, LTD.
HAMMONDSPORT, N.Y. 14840. ALCOHOL 11% BY VOLUME.
CONTAINS SULFITES

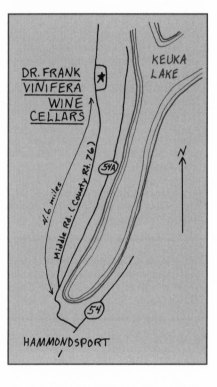

Dr. Konstantin Frank is undoubtedly the patriarch of all vinifera grape growing in the eastern United States. His contributions to winemaking are discussed on page 23 of this book. When he died in 1985 at the age of eighty-six, Vinifera Wine Cellars came under the capable management of his son Willy Frank. Son-in-law Walter Volz continues as vineyard manager, and vine grafting is still performed at their commercial nursery.

Dr. Frank's greatest interest lay in grape growing experiments; Willy Frank has chosen to concentrate on the production of fine wines. Willy markets his wines in New York City, Europe, and Japan, and intends to prove that the Finger Lakes make world class wines. Aware that the cool growing season here produces the more acidic grapes required for fine Champagne, Willy recently founded Chateau Frank, producing only *methode champenoise* sparkling wine. Chateau Frank Champagne, made from the classic French champagne grapes Chardonnay, Pinot Noir, and Pinot Meunier, has received national acclaim including several medals.

Willy is concerned that local wineries are victims of neglect from the New York City media. He believes that limited mention of New York State wines keeps them from achieving the recognition they deserve; indeed, he reports that he ships more wine to Tokyo than to Manhattan. But he finds satisfaction in the increasing number of interested and knowledgeable winery visitors.

DR. FRANK'S VINIFERA WINE CELLARS

Middle Road, Hammondsport, NY 14840
Phone: (607) 868-4884

OWNERS: The Frank and Volz families

WINEMAKERS: Peter Bell and Mark Veraguth

ESTABLISHED:
Property purchased 1953
First planting 1953
First vintage 1962

PRODUCTION:
70 acres planted
70 acres in production
18,000 gallon yield
Grapes are neither purchased nor sold.

GRAPES GROWN: Ten varieties of vinifera grapes grown.

WINES PRODUCED:
Dr. Frank's Vinifera Wine Cellars label:
Chardonnay
Estate White–*a blend of Chardonnay and Riesling*
Johannisberg Riesling
Gewurztraminer
Rkatsiteli
Muscat Ottonel
Premier Blush–*a blend of Pinot Noir, Chardonnay, and Riesling*
Pinot Noir
Cabernet Sauvignon
Chateau Frank label (made at Chateau Frank, next door):
Chateau Frank Champagne–*a sparkling wine made from Chardonnay, Pinot Noir, and Pinot Meunier*

RECENT AWARDS:
Consistently receive numerous awards, including:
1986 Chateau Frank Champagne–*five silver medals in 1991*

PRICING:
$4 to $22 per bottle; case discounts available.
Credit cards accepted.

AVAILABILITY:
Throughout New York, and in Connecticut, Massachusetts, Texas, Virginia, Washington, Washington D.C., Canada, and Japan.

TASTINGS AND TOURS:
Open all year, Monday through Saturday, 9 AM to 5 PM; Sunday, 1 PM to 5 PM.
$1.00 charge for tastings, refunded with purchase.
Tours available for groups by appointment.

CANA VINEYARDS WINERY

Cana Vineyards Winery takes its name from the biblical story of the marriage at Cana, where Christ turned water into wine. Owners Thomas and Anne Kiley Pellechia, believing in the marriage of food and wine, specialize in table wines intended to be served with a meal.

Anne and Thomas are media professionals transplanted from New York City to the woods overlooking Keuka Lake. Thomas gained winemaking experience using the grapes growing on their property. At present they purchase all of their grapes, focusing their energies on winemaking.

Having tasted wines from around the world, the Pellechias are familiar with international standards for each wine they make. They are also aware of Finger Lakes wines' particular characteristics, the results of a short growing season and cold winter. With this in mind, Thomas and Anne strive to produce wines with true varietal character. At the same time, they wish to reduce the mystique of wine, and make quality table wine a part of people's everyday lives.

To this end the Pellechias organize wine and food seminar weekends, with a lecture, a special dinner matching foods and wines, and an overnight stay at a local bed & breakfast. Thomas also leads a class which explores the components of wine, wine tasting, and the matching of wines and food. The class meets over dinners at various Albany restaurants.

The Pellechias are pleased with their wine offering and intend to continue producing five white wines. Wine sales are increasing as more people become aware of their winery, so they intend to renovate the winery to provide additional space for the increasing number of visitors. Soon they will add a second tasting bar. Unable to meet the current demand for their wines, Thomas and Anne are actively seeking capital for an extensive expansion of their facilities.

They personally conduct the wine tastings in the small, bright tasting room. A blackboard over the tasting counter offers food recommendations for each Cana wine. Contact the winery for the dates and details of their seminars.

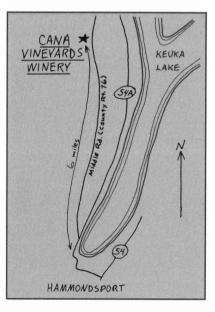

CANA VINEYARDS WINERY

9976 County Route 76, Hammondsport, NY 14840
Phone: (607) 868-4851

OWNERS: Thomas and Anne Kiley Pellechia

WINEMAKER: Thomas Pellechia

ESTABLISHED: Property purchased 1984
First vintage 1985

PRODUCTION: 2,000 gallon yield
All grapes are purchased.

WINES PRODUCED: Chardonnay
Proprietor's Reserve—*a blend that changes each vintage*
Johannisberg Riesling
Gewurztraminer
Vignoles

RECENT AWARDS: No longer enter competitions.

PRICING: $6.50 to $11.00 per bottle; case discounts available.
MasterCard and Visa accepted.

AVAILABILITY: At some local restaurants and liquor stores, and at a few in the Albany area.
Will ship UPS throughout New York State.

TASTINGS AND TOURS: Open May through October, Monday through Saturday, 10:30 AM to 5 PM;
Sunday, noon to 5 PM.
Open April and November, Saturday 10:30 to 5 PM; Sunday, noon to 5 PM.
$1.50 charge for tastings.
Tours are not available.

HUNT COUNTRY VINEYARDS

Joyce and Art Hunt were offered an opportunity to get away from desk jobs and jumped at the chance. Art's family, Finger Lakes farmers for six generations, let Art and Joyce plant and nurture grapes for six years and then purchase the family farm with the proceeds from their grape sales. Encouraged by the quality of the farm's location, its proximity to Keuka Lake, the benevolent lake effect weather, and the strong grape market, they chose to concentrate entirely on grape farming. Caught by surprise when the market softened, they adapted by selling to home winemakers and starting their own winery.

The Hunts grow native American, hybrid, and some vinifera grapes, as well as seedless table grapes. Their vineyards are noted as the site of the first successful field grafting experiment performed with

Thomas Zabadel, a Cooperative Extension grape specialist. Up until this point, grafting in this climate had only been done in temperature-controlled nurseries where the young rootstock and vines were joined, coated with paraffin, and incubated. In this experiment, grape vines were grafted onto already planted root stock. Field grafting has been a common procedure in warmer climates such as California, but special techniques are necessary for this colder climate. With this new procedure, several years and a lot of money can be saved in changing over fields from one grape variety to another.

Their latest venture, New York Wine Ship, was founded by the Hunts along with René and Nana Carrillo. Using trucks they've retrofitted themselves, they bring their own wines to New York City's Greenmarket and provide several wineries with efficient, cost-effective wine delivery to eastern New York State.

In October, the Hunts organize the Branchport Gourmet Harvest Festival. Held at their farm in conjunction with the Branchport community and area culinary students, they present grape stomping, winery tours, local artists, beautiful food displays, hay rides, a petting zoo, and pony rides.

The tasting room at Hunt Country Vineyards is a free-standing building near the vineyards. Recently expanded by enclosing the porch, the tasting room features triple sliding glass windows facing the vineyards. The lengthened tasting bar can accommodate increasing numbers of visitors. A display of gifts and custom gift baskets fill out the room. On summer Saturdays, hay rides through the vineyards are offered hourly.

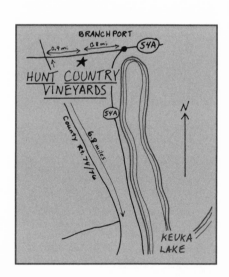

HUNT COUNTRY VINEYARDS

4021 Italy Hill Road, Branchport, NY 14418
Phone: (315) 595-2812

OWNERS: Art and Joyce Hunt

WINEMAKER: Art Hunt, Head Winemaker
Tim Benedict, Assistant Winemaker

ESTABLISHED: Property purchased 1979
First planting 1973
First vintage 1981

PRODUCTION:

70 acres planted
70 acres in production
30,000 gallon yield
Grapes and juice are sold.

GRAPES GROWN:

Aurore	DeChaunac	Seedless Table Grapes
Cayuga	Delaware	Seyval
Chancellor	Horizon	Vidal
Chardonnay	Niagara	Vignoles
Concord	Riesling	

WINES PRODUCED:

Chardonnay
Johannisberg Riesling
Seyval
Cayuga
Classic White–*a blend of Seyval, Cayuga, Vignoles, and Vidal*
Vignoles
Foxy Lady–*a blush wine blending Aurore, Delaware, and Colobel*
Classic Red–*a blend of DeChaunac, Chancellor, Baco Noir, and Colobel*
Late Harvest Ravat 51
Vidal Ice Wine

RECENT AWARDS: NV Classic Red–*1992 International Eastern Wine Competition, Bronze Medal*
NV Classic White–*1991 New York Wine & Food Classic, Silver Medal*
1991 Seyval Blanc–*1992 IEWC, Bronze Medal, 1992 San Diego National Wine
Competition, Bronze Medal*
1990 Cayuga–*1992 IEWC, Bronze Medal*
1989 Vignoles–*1991 NYW&FC, Silver Medal; 1990 IEWC, Bronze Medal*
1989 Johannisberg Riesling–*1990 IEWC, Bronze Medal*
1989 Vidal Ice Wine–*1992 Intervin, Gold Medal; 1992 IEWC, Gold Medal*

PRICING: $4.99 to $9.99 per bottle, Vidal Ice Wine $15.00 per half-bottle; case discounts.
MasterCard and Visa accepted.

AVAILABILITY: At liquor stores and restaurants throughout NYS, including NYC Greenmarket.

TASTINGS AND TOURS:

Open May through October, Monday through Saturday, 10 AM to 5 PM; Sunday,
noon to 5 PM.
Open April and November through Christmas, Saturday, 10 AM to 5 PM; Sunday,
noon to 5 PM, and by appointment.
$1.00 charge for tastings.
Informal tours available.
Hay wagon tour of vineyards on summer Saturdays, hourly 10 AM to 4 PM;
$1.50 per person, children under 10 free.

KEUKA SPRING VINEYARDS

KSV
1990

Keuka Spring

Chardonnay

Finger Lakes

A Dry White Wine • Oak Aged • Alcohol 13% by volume.
Produced & Bottled by Keuka Spring Cellars,
Penn Yan, N.Y. • Contains Sulfites

Len Wiltberger was a long-time amateur winemaker. He and his wife Judy were friends with many local grape growers and vintners and became intrigued by the potential of New York State as a major wine region, capable of producing world class wines. The Wiltbergers bought this property in 1981 to participate in the flowering of area winemaking.

Len and Judy shuttle between their home in Rochester, where Len works for Eastman Kodak, and the winery near Penn Yan. They are committed to the winery and somehow find the time to run the vineyards, winery, and tasting room. Theirs is a small boutique winery, producing award-winning white wines. They offer well-aged wines, often of older vintages. They're not in a hurry to release their wines, but choose to serve smooth, mature wines that won't require additional ageing.

The Wiltbergers plan to keep their operation small, offering premium wines in a pleasant atmosphere. They maintain moderate prices so people can enjoy wine as part of everyday life. Previously concentrating solely on white wines, they may add a red wine to their selection.

The winery is situated in a spacious white barn overlooking Keuka Lake. The tasting counter is set up on wine barrels, and the walls and ceiling are of rustic barn wood. A changing array of local artwork graces the walls. In the tasting room are several small stands with wine displays and snacks for purchase. There are picnic tables outside, and visitors are welcome to stroll through the vineyards.

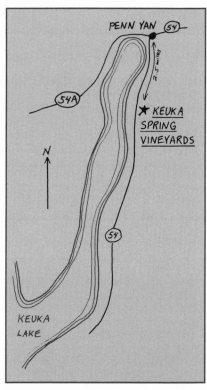

KEUKA SPRING VINEYARDS

Tasting room, 273 East Lake Road (Route 54), Penn Yan, NY 14527
Phone: (315) 536-4711
Business address, 50 Sugar Maple Drive, Rochester, NY 14615
Phone: (716) 621-4850

OWNERS: Len and Judy Wiltberger

WINEMAKER: Len Wiltberger

ESTABLISHED:
Property purchased 1981
First planting 1982
First vintage 1985

PRODUCTION:
6 acres planted
6 acres in production
2500 gallon yield
Grapes are both purchased and sold.

GRAPES GROWN:
Chardonnay
Riesling
Seyval
Vignoles

WINES PRODUCED:
Chardonnay
Seyval Blanc
Crooked Lake–*a blend of Seyval and Vignoles*
Riesling
Harvest White–*a blend of Cayuga, Seyval, and Riesling*
Harvest Blush–*a blend of Seyval, Vignoles, and Pinot Noir*
Vignoles
Crooked Lake Red–a blend of red wines

RECENT AWARDS: Have not entered competitions recently.

PRICING:
$5.49 to $9.49 per bottle; discounts available.
MasterCard and Visa accepted.

AVAILABILITY: Widely available in the Rochester area and in Finger Lakes area restaurants and liquor stores.

TASTINGS AND TOURS:
Open May and June, Saturday 10:30 AM to 5 PM; Sunday, noon to 5 PM.
Open July and August, Monday through Saturday,10:30 AM to 5 PM; Sunday, noon to 5 PM.
Open September and October, Monday, Friday and Saturday, 10:30 AM to 5 PM; Sunday, noon to 5 PM.
$1.00 charge for tastings.
Tours not available, although visitors are welcome to stroll the vineyards.

McGREGOR VINEYARD WINERY

Grape growing and home wine-making were originally a weekend avocation for the McGregors. From their 1971 start in a tent on their Keuka Lake hillside, the McGregors have built a thriving, well-respected farm winery. Along the way, their four children have lent a hand. Bob still has ties with Eastman Kodak in Rochester, but the family looks forward to ending over twenty years of commuting and to settling on their land.

The winery is located up an unpaved road that rises into the hills that surround Keuka Lake. The view is fabulous. Tastings are held on a deck overlooking the bluff and the lake below. Gentle wind chimes and hanging plants add to the atmosphere. When necessary, the tasting area annexes the nearby picnic tables, where a tent may be erected.

Early on, the McGregors were firmly committed to vinifera grapes. When they first planted, most local vineyards grew native American grapes such as Concord and Niagara, but the McGregors planted only vinifera and hybrid grapes and

were among the first in the area growing and using the red Pinot Noir grapes. They are the only winery, besides Dr. Frank's Vinifera Wine Cellars, growing and making wines from the Russian grapes Rkatsiteli, Saperavi, and Sereksia. These wines are so popular that Bob has recently planted more of the Russian grapes. His newest blend, Black Russian, is a deep-hued, robust wine of Saperavi and black Sereksia grapes.

McGregor's Clan Club is the core of their business. For an annual fee, club members receive bimonthly, specially priced "Clan Packs." These usually consist of two bottles, often including limited release and reserve wines. Club members also receive special discounts of case purchases, invitations to special events, and opportunities to purchase limited releases.

The McGregors hope to continue growing, with an annual production goal of 20,000 gallons. They offer a very extensive selection, catering to a variety of tastes. All the while, they resolve to grow the best grapes possible and produce premium wines.

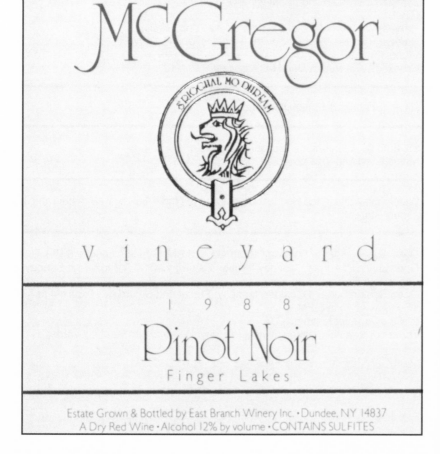

McGregor

SRIOGHAL MO DHREAM

v i n e y a r d

1 9 8 8

Pinot Noir

Finger Lakes

Estate Grown & Bottled by East Branch Winery Inc. • Dundee, NY 14837
A Dry Red Wine • Alcohol 12% by volume • CONTAINS SULFITES

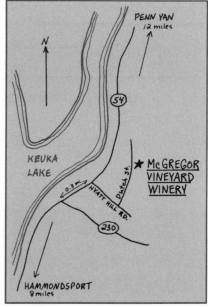

McGREGOR VINEYARD WINERY

5503 Dutch Street, Dundee, NY 14837
Phone: (607) 292-3999

OWNERS: Robert and Margaret McGregor

WINEMAKER: Robert McGregor

ESTABLISHED:
Property purchased 1971
First planting 1972
First vintage 1980

PRODUCTION:

28 acres planted
25 acres in production
12,000 gallon yield
Some grapes are purchased.

GRAPES GROWN:

Cayuga	Riesling
Chardonnay	Rkatsiteli
Gewurztraminer	Saperavi
Muscat Ottonel	Sereksia
Pinot Noir	Vignoles

WINES PRODUCED:

Blanc de Blancs–*a sparkling wine made from Chardonnay*	Seyval Blanc
	Cayuga
Sparkling Riesling	Vidal Blanc
Chardonnay	Verdelet
Chardonnay Reserve	Vignoles
Goodwin Hill Chardonnay	Pinot Noir Blanc
Alsatian Style Johannisberg Riesling	Gamay Beaujolais–*a nouveau-style wine*
Alsatian Style Gewurztraminer	Pinot Noir
Gewurztraminer	Reserve Pinot Noir
Johannisberg Riesling	Muscat Ottonel
Johannisberg Riesling Reserve	Sereksia
Keuka Highlands White–*a changing blend*	Bunch Select Johannisberg Riesling
	Late Harvest Gewurztraminer

RECENT AWARDS:
Consistently receive numerous awards, including:
1988 Goodwin Hill Chardonnay–*1990 San Francisco Fair, Silver Medal; 1991 Les Amis du Vin, Silver Medal; 1991 Intervin, Bronze Medal; 1990 Atlanta International Wine Festival, Bronze Medal; 1991 New York State Fair, Bronze Medal*
1988 Bunch Select Johannisberg Riesling–*1991 NYSF, Bronze Medal*
1988 Seyval Blanc–*1990 International Eastern Wine Competition, Bronze Medal*

PRICING:
$5.49 to $16.99 per bottle; quantity discounts available.
MasterCard and Visa accepted.

AVAILABILITY: At restaurants and some liquor stores throughout western New York State.

TASTINGS AND TOURS:

Open March through December, Monday through Saturday, 10 AM to 6 PM; Sunday, 11 AM to 5 PM.
Open January and February, daily, 11 AM to 4 PM.
$1.50 charge to taste three wines, extra charge for additional tastes.
Guided tours available.

WINEMAKING

Harvesting Grapes by Machine

Crusher and Press at Frontenac Point

Wine was most probably discovered thousands of years ago when the wild yeast growing on grapes caused some grape juice to ferment. Unlike most such accidental occurrences, however, this mishap had a happy consequence and produced a beverage which preserves itself and can be a delight to drink. Over time, winemaking has become a science and an art. While some wineries use high technology and produce millions of gallons of wine a year, there are many home winemakers making wine in five gallon batches in their basements.

The first step in winemaking is acquiring the fruit or the fruit juice. Grapes are crushed and pressed. To produce red wine, several days must pass between crushing and pressing to allow the grape skins to remain in contact with the juice; since most red grapes actually are light colored inside, the color of red wine comes from the skin. After pressing the grapes, yeast is added to the juice and allowed to ferment. When fermentation is complete and the solids settle out, the wine is "racked" or siphoned off the settled solids or lees. The wine is then per-

Pressing Grapes in a Vertical Press

mitted to stabilize in a cold environment, filtered as needed, and aged in stainless steel or oak casks. Finally it is bottled and aged further.

Wine can be initially aged in stainless steel tanks or oak barrels, although home winemakers often use large glass jugs, called carboys. Stainless steel and glass are nonpermeable and nonreactive, and thus do not alter the wine in any way. Oak contributes depth and body, and imparts rich, toasty flavors, sometimes with vanilla overtones. Oak can be overused, in which case the fruit is overwhelmed by oak flavors. Both the initial and bottle ageing permit the wine to become smoother as tannins convert to less astringent compounds. Additionally, the wine becomes more complex as subtle flavors emerge and the many component flavors blend together.

To make sparkling wine, the finished wine is transferred to a pressure resistant bottle, yeast and sugar to feed the yeast are added, the bottle is capped, and secondary fermentation occurs. Since the gases produced by this secondary fermentation cannot escape, they are absorbed into the wine and create the small bubbles for which champagne is famous. For *methode champenoise*, the remaining yeast solids are gradually shifted to the neck of the bottle and the sediment is "disgorged." This is accomplished by removing the cap while the bottle is upside down, then quickly

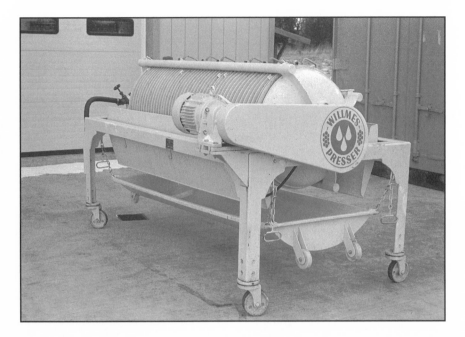

Horizontal Grape Press

Wine Filter

Waste from Crusher/Stemmer

Ageing Wine in Oak Barrels

Wine in Stainless Steel Tanks

Champagne Waiting for Disgorgement

righting it so only the sediment leaves the bottle. Some winemakers freeze the neck of the bottle before disgorgement to simplify the process. The bottle is topped off with a "dosage" of wine and sugar and then corked.

There is growing controversy over the use of sulfites in winemaking. The term "sulfites" actually covers an array of sulfur-based compounds, which are used in winemaking to protect the grapes from mold and rot, to sterilize equipment, and as a preservative in finished wines. Most winemakers and scientists agree that without the use of sulfites, wine cannot be aged and would go bad long before a good winemaker would even consider releasing his wines for consumption. Ancient Romans burned sulfur wicks in their empty wine casks, and sulfites are a natural result of fermentation; however, sulfites have a potential adverse effect, stimulating government agencies to require labels on wine, food, and drugs containing sulfites.

The science of winemaking begins before there are vines or fruit. Vineyard site selection, choice of rootstock, choice of varietal clone, grafting to the rootstock, pruning, protecting the fruit as it matures and the vines in winter all contribute to a wine's character. Even different methods of picking the grapes can influence the taste of a wine. The science extends to the exclusion of unwanted bacteria, molds, yeasts, oxygen, and anything else that will negatively affect the wine during fermentation and ageing.

The art of a fine winemaker includes the ability to capture the best of the grape's essence, to balance sugars and acids, to decide whether to age in oak and for how long, and to employ science in such a way to make the best wines possible.

SENECA LAKE WINERIES

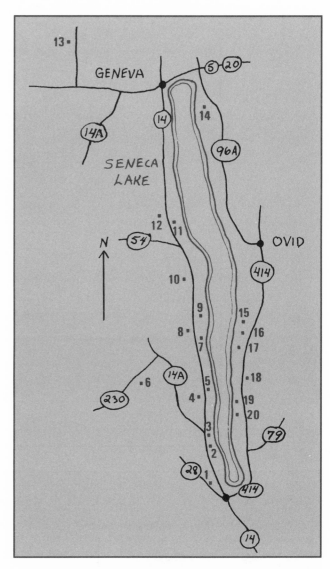

CASTEL GRISCH ESTATE WINERY

Castel Grisch

1990

Finger Lakes

Baco Noir

PRODUCED AND BOTTLED BY
CASTEL GRISCH WINERY
WATKINS GLEN, NEW YORK 14891 607-535-7711
CONTAINS SULFITES   ALCOHOL 11% BY VOL.

GOVERNMENT WARNING: (1) ACCORDING TO THE SURGEON GENERAL, WOMEN SHOULD NOT DRINK ALCOHOLIC BEVERAGES DURING PREGNANCY BECAUSE OF THE RISK OF BIRTH DEFECTS. (2) CONSUMPTION OF ALCOHOLIC BEVERAGES IMPAIRS YOUR ABILITY TO DRIVE A CAR OR OPERATE MACHINERY, AND MAY CAUSE HEALTH PROBLEMS.

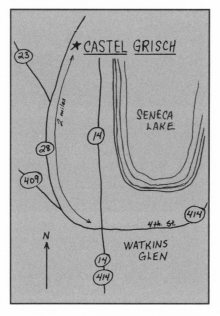

Swiss-born chemist Alois Baggenstoss has lived in the United States since the second World War. Upon retirement, Alois and Michelle Baggenstoss looked for a landscape similar to Switzerland and found their niche in the Finger Lakes. They found the high ridges over deep lakes and the snowy winters here much more satisfying than Florida, where they'd previously tried to retire. Here they started a small vineyard, built the manor, and opened first a winery and then a restaurant.

Up Irelandville Road high over Seneca Lake one finds the manicured estate of Castel Grisch. The tasting room and restaurant are at the end of a long driveway dotted with signs pointing out the different grape varieties and other items of interest. Tastings were previously held in the restaurant itself; recently a tasting room has been added off to one side.

The restaurant offers everything from a glass of wine for sipping on the terrace to a complete meal in the dining room. Those at Castel Grisch strive for a reasonably priced, casual restaurant with lovely decor and a magnificent view.

Early in 1992, Castel Grisch opened a new wine outlet in Hammondsport. In June 1992, Tom and Barbara Malina purchased Castel Grisch. They now offer overnight accommodations in the manor.

CASTEL GRISCH ESTATE WINERY

3380 County Road 28, Watkins Glen, NY 14891
Phone: (607) 535-9614

OWNER: Tom and Barbara Malina

WINEMAKER: Richard Evans

ESTABLISHED:
Property originally purchased 1982
Purchased by current owners 1992
First planting 1984
First vintage 1987

PRODUCTION:
23 acres planted
23 acres in production
12,000 gallon yield
Some grapes are purchased; grapes are sold.

GRAPES GROWN:
Chardonnay
Gewurztraminer
Riesling

WINES PRODUCED:
Blanc de Blanc–*a sparkling wine made from Chardonnay*
Chardonnay
French Chablis–*a blend of Chardonnay and Seyval*
Johannisberg Riesling
Gewurztraminer
Seyval Blanc
Catawba
Seneca Blush–*a blend of Seyval and Baco Noir*
Burgundy–*a blend of Baco Noir and Chardonnay*
Baco Noir

RECENT AWARDS: Have yet to enter competitions.

PRICING:
$4.20 to $11.00 per bottle; case discounts available.
MasterCard and Visa accepted.

AVAILABILITY:
At local restaurants and liquor stores.
UPS shipping available.

TASTINGS AND TOURS:
Open April through December, daily, 10 AM to 10 PM.
No charge for tastings.
Tours available by appointment.

LAKEWOOD VINEYARDS

Lakewood Vineyards is truly a family operation. They've been growing grapes ever since Monty Stamp's father purchased the property in 1952. After thirty-six years of grape growing, the Stamps have combined their expertise—Monty as a grower, Beverly in winery-related public relations, and son Chris as a professional winemaker—and opened a winery. Beverly worked for the New York State Wine Grape Growers and is a founding member of Women for NYS Wines, a promotional group for New York wines. Chris was an enologist (wine scientist) for Ohio University's grape program and helped out wineries

throughout Ohio. His younger brother David has a degree in plant science and manages the vineyard work as well as lending a hand at the winery. The family gets additional support from Bev's and Monty's siblings and their sons'

wives. Elizabeth Stamp (Chris' wife) is very active in the sales room.

Lakewood presently offers eleven wines, using vinifera, hybrid, and labrusca grapes. They work toward capturing the true varietal character of each grape. Catering to a variety of tastes, they produce both dry table wines and sweeter sipping wines.

In winter, the Stamps organize wine-and-food-pairing dinners. In conjunction with a local restaurant, they offer a multi-course dinner at the winery with a different wine matched to each course. Seating is limited; call the winery for details. Lakewood's friendly newsletter announces such events.

This modern winery is light and airy, with a cathedral ceiling, many windows, and an outdoor observation deck. The view reaches over the vineyards down to the lake's far side. In this promising location, just three miles north of Watkins Glen, the Stamps look forward to an ongoing, successful business that will keep the family together and provide a bright future for generations.

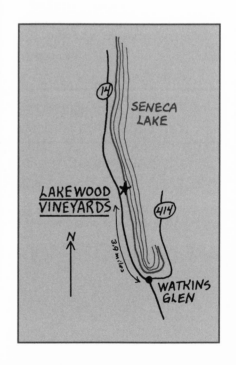

LAKEWOOD VINEYARDS

4024 Route 14, Watkins Glen, NY 14891
Phone: (607) 535-9252

OWNERS: Monty and Bev Stamp

WINEMAKERS: Chris Stamp

ESTABLISHED:
Property purchased 1951
First planting 1952
First vintage 1988

PRODUCTION:
53 acres planted
51 acres in production
8,500 gallon yield
Grapes are sold.

GRAPES GROWN:

Aurore	Chardonnay	Niagara
Catawba	Concord	Riesling
Cayuga	Delaware	Vignoles

WINES PRODUCED:
Chardonnay
Riesling
Cayuga
Long Stem White—*a blend of Cayuga and Vignoles*
Vignoles
Pink Catawba
Niagara
Delaware
Long Stem Red—*a blend of Baco Noir and Chancellor*
Pinot Noir
Glaciovinam—*a Delaware ice wine*

RECENT AWARDS:
1990 Niagara—*1991 International Eastern Wine Competition, Gold Medal*
1990 Pink Catawba—*1991 IEWC, Silver Medal*
1989 Riesling—*1990 IEWC, Silver Medal*
1989 Long Stem White—*1990 IEWC, Bronze Medal; 1990 American Wine Society, Bronze Medal*
1989 Delaware—*1991 NYW&FC, Bronze Medal*
1989 Long Stem Red—*1990 AWS, Bronze Medal*
1989 Cayuga White—*1990 AWS, Bronze Medal*
1989 Vignoles—*1990 NYW&FC, Bronze Medal*
1989 Pink Catawba—*1990 NYW&FC, Bronze Medal*
Finger Lakes Finest Grape Juice—*1990 New York Wine & Food Classic, Silver Medal*

PRICING:
$4.99 to $9.99 per bottle; case discounts available.
MasterCard, Visa, and Discover Card accepted.

AVAILABILITY: At restaurants and liquor stores throughout central New York.

TASTINGS AND TOURS:
Open May through December, Monday through Saturday, 10 AM to 5:30 PM; Sunday, noon to 6 PM.
Open January through April, Friday and Saturday, 10 AM to 5:30 PM; Sunday, noon to 5 PM; weekdays by appointment.
Informal tours available.

GIASI WINERY

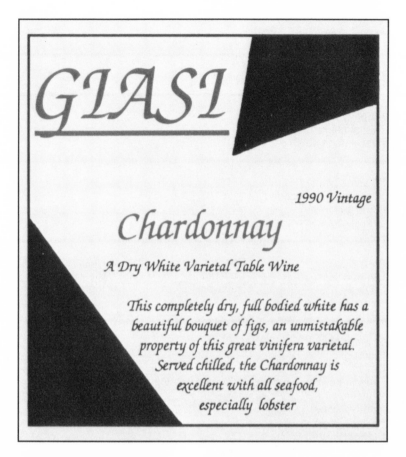

GIASI

1990 Vintage

Chardonnay

A Dry White Varietal Table Wine

This completely dry, full bodied white has a beautiful bouquet of figs, an unmistakable property of this great vinifera varietal. Served chilled, the Chardonnay is excellent with all seafood, especially lobster

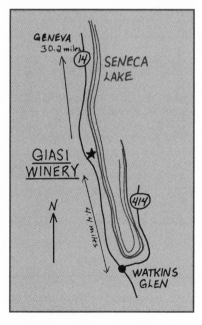

The Giasi family has made wine for generations, first in Italy and now here in the Finger Lakes. Winery founder Michael Giasi, whose father arrived here from southern Italy in 1910, was American-born.

In an unusual move, Michael took the three hybrid red grapes he chose to grow and planted them mixed together; when the grapes are harvested, the three grape varieties are thus always combined, and the winery's several distinct red wines differ only in the winemaking process. Many of these blended red wines have in common an Italian robustness unique in the Finger Lakes.

When Michael passed away in 1986, his wife Vera and their children carried on the tradition. This is truly a family operation. Vera handles the business and runs the tasting room. Son Paul is the winemaker, son Michael manages the vineyards, and Christina and Joseph help out wherever they can.

The tasting room is cool and inviting, with stained-glass windows, red carpets, and Tudor-style walls. Visitors may picnic on the deck outdoors. Vera Giasi often personally hosts tastings and willingly shares her thorough knowledge of the wines. Firmly committed to the winery, the Giasi family has increased the amount of wine made, has expanded distribution, and looks forward to continued growth.

GIASI WINERY

Route 14, Rock Stream, NY 14878
Phone: (607) 535-7785

OWNER: Vera Giasi

WINEMAKER: Paul Giasi

ESTABLISHED:
Property purchased 1972
First planting 1972
First vintage 1979

PRODUCTION:

20 acres planted
20 acres in production
6,500 gallon yield
Some grapes are purchased.

GRAPES GROWN:

Baco Noir
DeChaunac
Marechal Foch
Pinot Noir
Seyval

WINES PRODUCED:

Chardonnay
Riesling
Cayuga Blanc
Seyval Blanc
Watkins White—*a blend of Chardonnay, Seyval, and Cayuga*
Watkins Blush—*a blend of Cayuga and young red grapes*
Connubial—*a blush wine made from Seyval and young red grapes*
Vindametrix—*a blend of Pinot Noir, Baco Noir, Marechal Foch, and DeChaunac*
Convivial—*a blend of Pinot Noir, Baco Noir, Marechal Foch, and DeChaunac*
Watkins Red—*a blend of Pinot Noir, Baco Noir, Marechal Foch, and DeChaunac*
Paul's Red—*a blend of Pinot Noir, Baco Noir, Marechal Foch, and DeChaunac*
Connoisseur—*made from Pinot Noir*
Cherry—*made from Montmorency cherries*

RECENT AWARDS: Do not enter competitions.

PRICING:
$5.00 to $12.00 per bottle; case discounts available.
Credit cards are not accepted.

AVAILABILITY: In central New York liquor stores and restaurants.

TASTINGS AND TOURS:

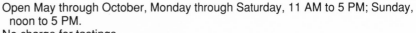

Open May through October, Monday through Saturday, 11 AM to 5 PM; Sunday,
  noon to 5 PM.
No charge for tastings.
Tours not available.

FULKERSON WINE CELLARS

FULKERSON

1989

FINGER LAKES TABLE WINE
CHARDONNAY

Produced & Bottled by Fulkerson Wine Cellars • Dundee • New York • 14837
CONTAINS SULFITES
Table Wine

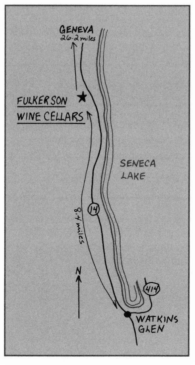

Among the earliest settlers in this area, the Fulkerson family arrived in the Finger Lakes in 1805 and their descendants are still here today. Sayre Fulkerson and his wife Nancy have lived here all their lives and twelve years ago bought their own farm.

A former assistant winemaker with Glenora Wine Cellars, Sayre and Nancy opened a juice plant at their farm in 1979. The Fulkersons grow grapes for wineries, press juice for home winemakers, and sell home winemaking equipment. They welcome inquiries from anyone interested in making their own wine. The Fulkersons are happy to offer advice and instruction. During September and October, they provide over 25 varieties of fresh grape juice.

After years of grape growing, helping home winemakers, and watching the success of the farm wineries, the Fulkersons had decided to make and sell their own wines. This is the very first winery in the world to offer wines made from the seedless table grapes Himrod, Lakemont, and Canadice, with which they have made complex dessert wines.

As a natural outgrowth of their juice business, they offer their wine for tasting and sale at their home winemakers' shop. They plan to grow slowly and keep the juice business their primary concern. They prefer keeping this a family operation and maintaining all aspects of their diversified business themselves.

FULKERSON WINE CELLARS

5576 Route 14, Dundee, NY 14837
Phone: (607) 243-7883, shop; (607) 243-8270, home

OWNERS: Sayre and Nancy Fulkerson

WINEMAKER: Sayre Fulkerson

ESTABLISHED: Property in the family since 1805, purchased 1980
Oldest planting 1929
First vintage 1988

PRODUCTION: 70 acres planted
70 acres in production
5,000 gallon yield
Grapes are both purchased and sold.

GRAPES GROWN:

Aurore	Gewurztraminer
Canadice–*a hybrid seedless table grape*	65.533.13–*a Gewurztraminer hybrid*
Catawba	Himrod–*a hybrid seedless table grape*
Cayuga	Lakemont–*a hybrid seedless table grape*
Chardonnay	
Concord	Niagara
DeChaunac	Riesling
Delaware	Seyval
Diamond	Vidal
Dutchess	Vignoles

WINES PRODUCED:
Chardonnay
Riesling
Gewurztraminer
Seyval
Cayuga
Vidal
Heritage White–*a blend of Vidal, Aurore, and Cayuga*
Delaware
Lakemont
Canadice
Matinée–*made from Himrod*
Rosé–*a blend of Diamond and Marechal Foch*
Reserve Red–*a blend of Chelois and Baco Noir*
Pinot Noir
Late Harvest Vignoles

RECENT AWARDS: 1989 Seyval–*1991 International Eastern Wine Competition, Silver Medal*
1989 Late Harvest Vignoles–*1991 IEWC, Bronze Medal*

PRICING: $5.00 to $10.00 per bottle; discounts available.
Credit cards not accepted.

AVAILABILITY: At selected local restaurants.

TASTINGS AND TOURS: Open May through November, daily, 9 AM to 5 PM.
$1.00 charge for tastings, refunded with purchase.
Informal tours upon request.

GLENORA WINE CELLARS

Glenora Wine Cellars was one of the first wineries to open under the Farm Winery Act of 1976 and the first Finger Lakes winery to be built from the ground up since Prohibition. In 1987, the winery launched a major expansion focusing on *methode champenoise* sparkling wines and premium table wines.

Most grapes are purchased from the founding owners and other grape growers. Feeling that the quality of the grapes makes the wine, Glenora has maintained close ties with local grape growers and has recently purchased 35 acres of vineyards.

President Gene Pierce believes that as the vines in this region mature they will produce complex, world class wines. The people at Glenora Wine Cellars aim to fulfill this region's potential. They recognize this area as a prime sparkling wine region and in 1980 began by making 100 cases of such wine. Today they are one of the largest producers of *methode champenoise*

sparkling wine on the east coast. They also produce Riesling, Chablis-style Chardonnay and other varietals. They hope to take the company from a regional winery to a nationally known company. Mr. Pierce believes they have built a name, deliver consistent quality, and produce the quantity necessary to distribute beyond New York State's boundaries.

The winery is situated on a hill overlooking Seneca Lake, and has a very large tasting room with cathedral ceilings, exposed wooden trusses, numerous picture windows, and a large deck. Glenora hosts numerous events, from boat races on the lake to jazz concerts at the winery. Their annual Leaves & Lobster festival in September celebrates the Finger Lakes fall foliage with a New England-style lobster bake. Private events out of season and Sunday brunches in winter take advantage of Glenora's extensive facilities. The well-staffed tasting room efficiently handles the many visiting tourists. Wine related items and other gifts are available for purchase.

GLENORA

1990

FINGER LAKES

JOHANNISBERG
RIESLING

PRODUCED AND BOTTLED BY
GLENORA WINE CELLARS, INC., DUNDEE,
NEW YORK 14837 USA

ALCOHOL 10.5% BY VOLUME

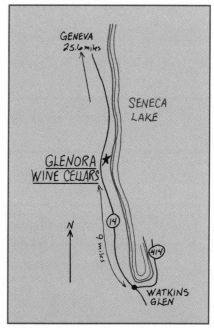

GLENORA WINE CELLARS

Glenora-on-Seneca, Route 14, Dundee, NY 14837
Phone: (607) 243-5511

OWNERS: Gene Pierce, John Potter, Ed Dalrymple
Gene Pierce, Winery President

WINEMAKER: David Munksgard, Head Winemaker

ESTABLISHED: Property purchased 1977
First vintage 1977
Vineyard purchased 1990

PRODUCTION: 35 acres planted
35 acres in production
150,000 gallon yield
Grapes are purchased.

WINES PRODUCED:

Glenora label:
Blanc de Blancs–*a sparkling wine made from Chardonnay, Pinot Noir, and Pinot Blanc*
Brut Chardonnay–*a sparkling wine made from Chardonnay*
Chardonnay
Chardonnay Reserve
Dry Riesling
Johannisberg Riesling
Gewurztraminer
Fume Blanc–*made from Sauvignon Blanc Cayuga*
Seyval Blanc
Blush–*a blend of Seyval, Baco Noir, and Pinot Noir*
Merlot
Cabernet Sauvignon
Trestle Creek label:
Chardonnay
Trestle Creek–*a blend of Cayuga and Seyval*

RECENT AWARDS: New York Winery of the Year–*1991 New York Wine & Food Classic*
1988 Blanc de Blancs–*1991 San Francisco Fair, Double Gold Medal; 1991 NYW&FC, Silver Medal*
1990 Johannisberg Riesling–*1991 American Wine Competition, Gold Medal; 1991 New York State Fair, Silver Medal*
1990 Dry Riesling–*1991 NYSF, Gold Medal*
1989 Johannisberg Riesling–*1991 NYW&FC, Silver Medal; 1991 International Eastern Wine Competition, Silver Medal*
1989 Dry Riesling–*1991 NYW&FC, Silver Medal*
1988 Chardonnay Reserve–*1991 IEWC, Gold Medal; 1991 NYSF, Silver Medal*
1987 Brut–*1991 NYW&FC, Gold Medal*
Numerous other awards have been received.

PRICING: $4.99 to $13.99 per bottle, case discounts available.
MasterCard and Visa accepted.

AVAILABILITY: Available throughout New York State and 12 other states

TASTINGS AND TOURS:

Open year round, Monday through Saturday, 10 AM to 5 PM; Sunday, noon to 5 PM.
Closed Easter, Thanksgiving, Christmas, and New Year's Day.
No charge for tastings.
Tour consists of audiovisual presentations and tasting.

BARRINGTON CHAMPAGNE COMPANY

Barrington
CHAMPAGNE CO.

Blanc de Blancs
METHODE CHAMPENOISE

**FINGER LAKES CHAMPAGNE PRODUCED & BOTTLED BY
THE BARRINGTON CHAMPAGNE CO.
DUNDEE, NEW YORK 14837   ALC. 12% by vol.**

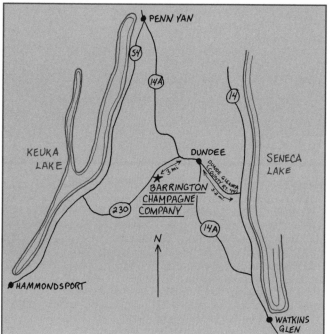

Ray Spencer is the owner, not only of the Barrington Champagne Company, but of the Red Brick Inn and Crystal Spring Water Company as well. Previously a manager and winemaker for Glenora Wine Cellars, Ray began his own champagne production in 1982 and purchased the Red Brick Inn in 1984. The Crystal Springs, which supported a health resort in the late 1800's, flow a mile from the Inn.

On a visit to France, Ray was inspired by a small champagne producer housed in a grand old chateau with cellars brimming over with champagne. Ray couldn't purchase even a single bottle because long-standing customers had already spoken for every bottle of champagne. He returned to the States and turned this vision into the Barrington Champagne Company and Red Brick Inn.

The four bedrooms at the Red Brick Inn reflect Ray's inspiration in their wine motifs: the Chablis, Champagne, Burgundy, and Bordeaux rooms. On the first floor is a large country kitchen, a formal living room, dining room, and, Ray hopes, a library. The winery is found in the cellar, where Ray produces a limited quantity of *methode champenoise* sparkling wines. Purchasing choice chardonnay and pinot noir grapes, he unstintingly bottle-ages the wines to produce those qualities found in the world's finest champagnes.

The winery is open by appointment only. The Inn is open year round. Crystal Spring Water can be found on many supermarket shelves.

BARRINGTON CHAMPAGNE COMPANY

2081 Route 230, Dundee, NY 14837
Phone: (607) 243-8844

OWNER:	Ray Spencer
WINEMAKER:	Ray Spencer
ESTABLISHED:	Property purchased 1984 First vintage 1982
PRODUCTION:	1,000 gallon yield All grapes are purchased
WINES PRODUCED:	Blanc de Blancs–*a sparkling wine made from Chardonnay and Pinot Noir* Crémant–*a creamier, softer sparkling wine made from Chardonnay* Reserve–*a sparkling wine made from Pinot Noir and Chardonnay* Blanc de Noir–*a sparkling wine made from Pinot Noir*
RECENT AWARDS:	Included in Pierce's Annual New York State Barrel Dinner, 1988 and 1989
PRICING:	$12.00 to $18.00 per bottle. Credit cards not accepted.
AVAILABILITY:	Only at the winery and at three area restaurants.
TASTINGS AND TOURS:	By appointment only. Red Brick Inn Bed and Breakfast open year round.

SQUAW POINT WINERY

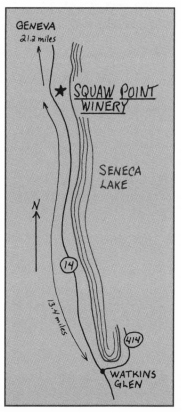

The way to Squaw Point Winery is heralded by "barrel people"—figures with wine barrel torsos and white tubular limbs. These "barrel-chested" figures are active, tilling the field with a coopered wooden horse, picnicking, and pointing the way to the winery. With this bit of craftsmanship, Squaw Point seems to have solved the problems of what to do with wooden barrels no longer suitable for ageing wine and how to advertise the winery very effectively.

David Miles' family has owned this property for years. Grapes have grown here since 1866. Most of the old vineyards are so tangled that David buys his grapes from other local growers, which leaves him time to focus on winemaking and marketing. Besides the winery, he has a retail outlet in Newark, north of the lakes, and one in Watkins Glen's Seneca Market. These, too, are flanked by the unmistakable barrel people.

Using vinifera, hybrid, and native American grapes, David produces a broad variety of wines. He's currently working on some drier wines. His wife Clarice runs the tasting room. Annually, they hold a wine auction and barbeque.

Some of the Squaw Point wines are labeled with a reproduction of a label used there in the 1800's on crates of grapes sent off to urban markets. It shows a view of the old grape packing house, which burned down some time ago.

A new barn holds both the winery and tasting room, where antique wine paraphernalia is displayed and modern items are for sale. Outdoors, a ninety-foot walk-up windmill provides a spectacular view. Visitors are welcome to stroll the vineyards and lunch in the nearby picnic area.

SQUAW POINT WINERY

Poplar Point Road, Dundee, NY 14837
Phone: (607) 243-8602

OWNER: David Miles

WINEMAKER: David Miles

ESTABLISHED: Property purchased 1986
First vintage 1986

PRODUCTION:  2 acres planted
0 acres in production
10,000 gallon yield
All grapes are purchased.

WINES PRODUCED: Golden Mystique–*a 100% varietal champagne with a secret ingredient*
Chardonnay
Riesling
Seyval
Cayuga White
Morning Mist–*a blend of Chardonnay, Cayuga, and Seyval*
Moonglow–*a blend of Cayuga and Seyval*
Spice–*Moonglow with spice essences, intended to be served warm*
Sweetheart–*a blend of Niagara and Cayuga*
Amity–*a blend of Leon Millot, DeChaunac, and Cayuga*
Cabo–*a blend of Leon Millot, DeChaunac, Cayuga, and Seyval*
Irby–*a blend of Colobel and DeChaunac*
Leon & Friends–*a blend of Leon Millot, Colobel, Baco Noir, and Marechal Foch*
Ravat Brix Late Harvest
Vidal Ice Wine

RECENT AWARDS: 1990 Ravat Brix Late Harvest–*1991 New York State Fair, Silver Medal*
1989 Cabo–*1990 Intervin, Bronze Medal*

PRICING: $4.98 to $9.98 per bottle; discounts available.
MasterCard and Visa accepted.

AVAILABILITY: In Squaw Point's own retail shops in Newark and Watkins Glen, in the New York
City Greenmarket, and in very limited local distribution.

TASTINGS AND TOURS: Open May through October, Monday through Saturday, 10 AM to 5 PM;
Sunday, noon to 5 PM.
Open November, Saturday, 10 AM to 5 PM; Sunday, noon to 5 PM.
Open December through April for sales only; no tastings.
$0.50 charge to taste five wines; or $2.50 charge to taste five wines and receive
souvenir wine glass.
Tours not available, although visitors are welcome to stroll the grounds.

HERMANN J. WIEMER VINEYARD

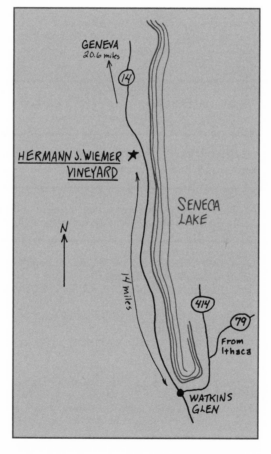

Hermann Wiemer can trace his heritage through a three hundred year line of German winemakers. He came to this country in 1968 to serve as head winemaker for a local winery. Satisfied with the grape-growing potential of the Finger Lakes, Wiemer purchased a farm and set up his own winery, vineyard, and nursery.

Here on Seneca Lake, Wiemer not only cultivates and produces high quality vinifera grapes and wines, but grafts vinifera grape vines for sale throughout the United States. He utilizes the most modern technology to yield the finest grapes, employing a new mechanical harvester from France which doesn't damage the vines the way the older ones tended to do.

Wiemer has been highly acclaimed for his German-style wines. His winery is often the first one mentioned when people speak of high quality Finger Lakes wines. Wiemer wines range in sweetness from a quite dry Chardonnay to the opulent Bunch Select Late Harvest Riesling. For the winery's tenth anniversary, they produced a *methode champenoise* sparkling Blanc de Noir. Wiemer released their first reserve Chardonnay, and the 1990 harvest encouraged them to make a lighter, Auslese-style late harvest Riesling.

Wiemer wine is served by Royal Viking Cruises. It is among the few Finger Lakes wines to penetrate the New York City market, where it is available at many fine restaurants.

The winery, housed in a renovated Victorian barn, includes a small but airy tasting area. Visitors are encouraged to tour the winery and vineyards, guided by a map and printed information.

HERMANN J. WIEMER VINEYARD

Route 14, Dundee, NY 14837
Phone: (607) 243-7971

OWNER: Hermann J. Wiemer

WINEMAKER: Dana Keeler

ESTABLISHED:
Property purchased 1973
First planting 1973
First vintage 1979

PRODUCTION:

75 acres planted
75 acres in production
31,000 gallon yield
Grafted vines are sold.

GRAPES GROWN:

Chardonnay
Gamay Noir
Gewurztraminer
Pinot Noir
Riesling

WINES PRODUCED:

Champagne Naturel–*100% Riesling*
Blanc de Noir–*a sparkling wine made from Chardonnay and Pinot Noir*
Chardonnay
Chardonnay Reserve
Wiemer Vinifera White–*a blend of Riesling, Chardonnay, and Gewurztraminer*
Dry Johannisberg Riesling
Johannisberg Riesling (semi-dry)
Pinot Noir
Late Harvest Johannisberg Riesling
Individual Bunch Select Late Harvest Riesling

RECENT AWARDS:
1990 Dry Johannisberg Riesling–*1992 National Orange Show, Silver Medal*
1987 Individual Bunch Select Late Harvest Riesling–*1992 NOS, Gold Medal*

PRICING:
$5.49 to $18.99 per bottle; discounts available.
MasterCard, Visa, and American Express accepted.

AVAILABILITY:
Available throughout New York, and in California, Connecticut, Maryland, Massachusetts, Minnesota, New Hampshire, North Carolina, Pennsylvania, and Washington, D.C.

TASTINGS AND TOURS:

Open May through November, Monday through Saturday, 10 AM to 5 PM; Sunday, 11 AM to 5 PM.
Open April, Monday through Friday, 10 AM to 5 PM; Saturday, noon to 5 PM.
Open January through March by appointment only.
No charge for tastings.
Self-guided tours are available; private tours by appointment only.

FOUR CHIMNEYS FARM WINERY

Four Chimneys is the only organic winery in the Finger Lakes, and one of the few in the United States. Founded by Walter Pedersen and Scott Smith, the winery is now run by the Four Chimneys community. They have done away with chemical insecticides, herbicides, and fertilizers, and rely instead on insect predators and herbal and vegetable sprays. Seeking to produce healthy soil, grapevines, and wine–and ultimately a healthier world–they also avoid many of the chemical additives available to winemakers.

The winery attempts to please many palates, producing over twenty wines in American, French, and German styles. Local cheeses and other foods are available for purchase. The elegantly restored Victorian barn is fitted out with a piano and small stage, the setting for the chamber music concert series offered on Saturday nights in July, August, and September. A special seven-course dinner follows each concert; reservations are necessary.

Four Chimneys recently opened the Gold Coast (La Côte d'Or), just up Hall Road on Route 14. This warm, elegant restaurant serves local seasonal cuisine, featuring organic vegetarian dishes as well as game meats and fish. Off season they plan to offer seven course dinners matching foods and wines.

Four Chimneys' wines have been available for several years at the New York City Greenmarket and local farmers markets. They now sell some wine to retailers. Their newest venture, Four Chimneys Organic Selections, imports and distributes certified organic wines from Europe.

Four Chimneys' Scandinavian Festival, a traditional summer solstice celebration, is held on the Saturday nearest June 24. Visitors enjoy Scandinavian foods, dance, live music, crafts, and ethnic-style wines. Call ahead for details.

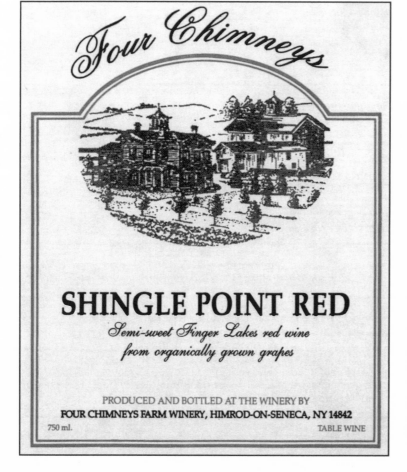

Four Chimneys

SHINGLE POINT RED

*Semi-sweet Finger Lakes red wine
from organically grown grapes*

PRODUCED AND BOTTLED AT THE WINERY BY
FOUR CHIMNEYS FARM WINERY, HIMROD-ON-SENECA, NY 14842

750 ml.   TABLE WINE

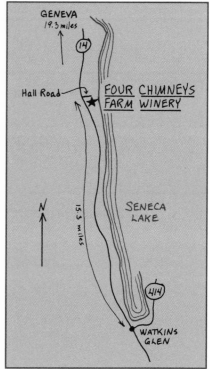

FOUR CHIMNEYS FARM WINERY

RD 1, Hall Road, Himrod, NY 14842
Phone: (607) 243-7502

OWNER: Four Chimneys Farm Winery Trust

WINEMAKER: Scott Smith

ESTABLISHED:
Property purchased 1976
First planting 1976
First vintage 1980

PRODUCTION:
80 acres planted
70 acres in production
15,000 gallon yield
A limited amount of grapes is purchased.

GRAPES GROWN:
Aurore
Baco Noir
Cabernet Sauvignon
Catawba
Chardonnay
Concord
DeChaunac
Gewurztraminer
Muscat
Niagara
Pinot Gris
Pinot Noir
Riesling
Seyval Blanc
Vidal

WINES PRODUCED:
Brut Champagne–*made from Seyval*
Special Reserve Chardonnay
Dry Riesling
Seyval Blanc
Kingdom White–*made from Aurore*
Dayspring–*a German-style wine, blended from five grapes*
Golden Crown–*made from Diamond*
Eye of the Dove–*a rosé wine made from Baco Noir*
Eye of the Bee–*a rosé wine made from Concord with honey*
Premier Nouveau–*a nouveau-style wine made from Baco Noir*
Kingdom Red–*a changing blend of DeChaunac and Baco Noir*
Special Reserve Kingdom Red–*a changing blend of DeChaunac, Rougeon, and Baco Noir*
Shingle Point Red–*a changing blend of late harvest red grapes*
Late Harvest Vignoles
Late Harvest Delaware
Special Select Reserve–*a dessert wine made from Aurore*
Aurora
Mead
Apple Wine
Raspberry Sunrise–*a blend of raspberries and a neutral red wine*
Blueberry Skies–*a blend of blueberries and a neutral red wine*
Strawberry Meadows–*a blend of strawberries and a neutral red wine*
Celestial Peach–*a blend of peaches and a neutral white wine*

RECENT AWARDS:	Rarely enter competitions.

PRICING:	$5.95 to $16.95 per bottle. Credit cards are not accepted.

AVAILABILITY:	At liquor stores throughout the state and at local and New York City restaurants. UPS shipping available within New York State.

TASTINGS AND TOURS:

Open May through November, daily, 10 AM to 6 PM.
Open December through April, daily, 10 AM to 5 PM.
$1.00 charge for tastings, refunded with purchase.
Tours not available.

Chamber music concerts at 8:15 PM Saturdays in July, August, and September.
Wine tasting dinners before each concert; reservations required.
Gold Coast Restaurant (La Cote d'Or) open April through December.

PREJEAN WINERY

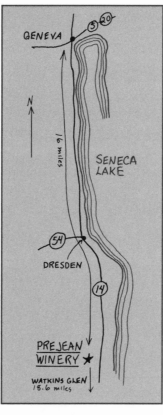

Prejean Winery, overlooking Seneca Lake, is housed in a rustic structure completed in 1986. The large tasting room with its scenic picture window adjoins the meticulously clean winery filled with stainless steel tanks and oak barrels.

Originally from West Virginia and New Orleans respectively, Elizabeth and Jim Prejean lived in California before moving East. Jim's visits to nearby Geneva for the American Can Company brought the Prejeans to the Finger Lakes grape growing region. They chose to move here and establish a vineyard and winery. Jim's recent death left Elizabeth and son Tom in charge of the entire operation.

Working closely with their winemaker, Jim Zimar, the Prejeans strive to produce quality, complex, dry wines from premium vinifera and hybrid cultivars. They are considering planting new vinifera red grapes. Prejean Winery continues to offer reasonably priced Chardonnays and has recently added a Merlot to their selection. Their dry Riesling and Gewurztraminer are now barrel-fermented in an Alsatian style to further distinguish them from their semi-dry versions of these wines.

Drawing on their family heritage, the Prejeans stage an annual Cajun Festival in August, featuring Cajun music and food. The winery's case club is dubbed "Prejean Cajuns." Club members enjoy special releases, limited quantity wines, special events, and a newsletter. The Prejeans intend to keep up with the demand for their wines and hope to firmly establish their sales to restaurants and liquor stores throughout New York State.

PREJEAN WINERY

2634 Route 14, Penn Yan, NY 14527
Phone: (315) 536-7524

OWNER: Elizabeth Prejean

WINEMAKER: Jim Zimar

ESTABLISHED: Property purchased 1978
First planting 1979
First vintage 1985

PRODUCTION: 37 acres planted
37 acres in production
11,000 gallon yield
Grapes are sold.

GRAPES GROWN: Cayuga
Chardonnay
Gewurztraminer
Marechal Foch
Merlot
Riesling
Vignoles

WINES PRODUCED: Chardonnay
Vintner's Reserve Chardonnay
Johannisberg Riesling, Dry (Barrel-Fermented)
Gewurztraminer, Dry (Barrel-Fermented)
Johannisberg Riesling, Semi-dry
Gewurztraminer, Semi-dry
Cayuga White
Proprietor's Red–*a blend of Marechal Foch and Chardonnay*
Marechal Foch
Merlot
Late Harvest Vignoles
Late Harvest Johannisberg Riesling

RECENT AWARDS: 1989 Johannisberg Riesling, Semi-Dry–*1991 American Wine Society,
Silver Medal*
1990 Dry Gewurztraminer (Barrel-Fermented)–*1991 Grand Harvest Award*
1990 Vintner's Reserve Chardonnay–*1991 Grand Harvest Award*

PRICING: $6.00 to $15.00 per bottle; discounts available.
MasterCard and Visa accepted.

AVAILABILITY: Throughout New York State, Illinois, and Ontario.

TASTINGS AND TOURS: Open May through November, Monday through Saturday, 10 AM to 5 PM;
Sunday, noon to 5 PM.
Open December through April, Monday through Saturday, 10 AM to 4 PM;
Sunday, noon to 4 PM.
Charge for tastings.
Tours not available.

ANTHONY ROAD WINE COMPANY

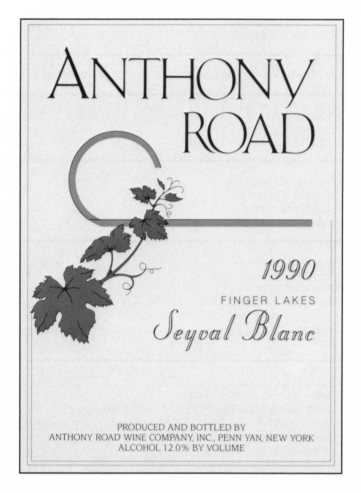

ANTHONY ROAD

1990

FINGER LAKES

Seyval Blanc

PRODUCED AND BOTTLED BY
ANTHONY ROAD WINE COMPANY, INC., PENN YAN, NEW YORK
ALCOHOL 12.0% BY VOLUME

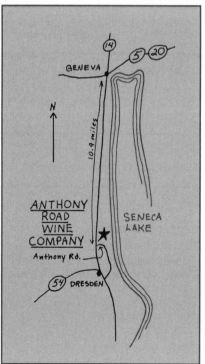

Twenty years ago, John and Ann Martini decided it would be fun to grow grapes and make wine. So, in 1973, they bought this farm, settled in, and planted grapes. Ann tends the 25-acre vineyard while John works at the New York Agricultural Experiment Station. They earned an excellent grape-growing reputation, but eventually gave up the idea of opening their own winery. In fact, they even considered ripping out the vineyards as grape selling became difficult.

Then in 1989 the Martinis got together with long-time friend Derek Wilber and his wife, Donna. Derek started working on grape farms at age 13, graduated Cornell University with a degree in pomology (fruit science), managed farms, practiced home winemaking, became winemaker for Finger Lakes Wine Cellars and then for Widmer's Wine Cellars. Together, the Martinis and Wilbers had all of the ingredients for a successful winery and Anthony Road Wine Company was born.

The people at Anthony Road Wine Company take pride in the wines they've made and look forward to planting more grapes and increasing the volume of wine produced. They try to compete on price and quality, offering well-made wines priced for everyday dining enjoyment.

The small winery houses both the tasting room and winemaking area, which can be viewed through windows from the tasting area. The wine press and other winemaking equipment flank the building. The winery's logo depicts the sun rising over nearby Seneca Lake.

ANTHONY ROAD WINE COMPANY

1225 Anthony Road, Penn Yan, NY 14527
Phone: (315) 536-2182

OWNERS: Ann and John Martini, Derek and Donna Wilber

WINEMAKER: Derek Wilber

ESTABLISHED:
Property purchased 1973
First planting 1973
First vintage 1989

PRODUCTION:

25 acres planted
25 acres in production
7,000 gallon yield
Grapes are sold and purchased.

GRAPES GROWN:

Aurore
Chardonnay
Riesling
Seyval
Vignoles

WINES PRODUCED:

Chardonnay
Riesling
Seyval
Vignoles
Vintner's Select–*a blend of Seyval, Riesling, and Vignoles*
Pinot Noir
Late Harvest Vignoles

RECENT AWARDS:
1989 Late Harvest Vignoles–*1991 International Eastern Wine Competition, Gold Medal*
1989 Vignoles–*1991 New York Wine & Food Classic, Gold Medal*
1989 Chardonnay–*1991 NYW&FC, Bronze Medal*
1989 Riesling–*1991 NYW&FC, Bronze Medal*

PRICING:
$5.00 to $10.00 per bottle; case discounts available.
MasterCard and Visa accepted.

AVAILABILITY: Available throughout New York State, and at the New York City Greenmarket.

TOURS AND TASTINGS:

Open May through November, Monday through Saturday, 10 AM to 5 PM;
Sunday, noon to 5 PM.
December through April, by appointment only.
$2.00 charge for tastings, includes souvenir wine glass.
Tours are not available.

FOX RUN VINEYARDS

The Wildricks became interested in wine more than twenty years ago, while visiting the California wine regions and the Finger Lakes. Living in New Jersey, they visited the Finger Lakes often and in 1980 decided to move here. They looked for land, studied geological and climatological maps, and pinpointed this particular farm. They were thrilled when it subsequently came on the market.

While living in Hammondsport, they planted vines, opened the Penn Yan farmhouse as a bed & breakfast (which is now their home), and transformed the barn into a winery. Preserving the pre-Civil War barn dictated the winery's design. The Wildricks had contractors shore up the foundation, add insulation, and put up new exterior siding. The light, airy tasting room with a stunning view over the lake is an addition that further strengthened the barn's foundation. The insulation and interior sandblasting yielded a good winemaking environment, which can be viewed through floor to ceiling windows from the tasting room.

The winery's hillside location provides a panoramic view of Seneca Lake, which can be enjoyed through the octagonal tasting room's large windows or from the spacious porch. Graced with stained glass, plank floors, and wooden beams, the tasting room displays crystal and dishes in antique china cabinets as well as gifts available for purchase.

The Wildricks have brought in long-time friend Jim Gifford as winemaker. Jim previously was employed at Great Western and Glenora Wine Cellars, and has his own winemaking consulting business. Fox Run strives for excellence, concentrating on producing a few wines. Their most recent wine, a French-style sparkling wine, is the joint product of Jim Gifford's expertise and Fox Run's well-placed vineyards. The Wildricks look forward to new plantings coming into production, the increasing maturity of their vineyards, and returning satisfied customers.

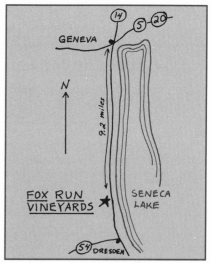

FOX RUN VINEYARDS

670 Route 14, Penn Yan, NY 14527
Phone: (315) 536-4616

OWNERS: Larry and Adele Wildrick

WINEMAKER: Jim Gifford

ESTABLISHED:
Property purchased 1983
First planting 1984
First vintage 1989

PRODUCTION:
27 acres planted
11 acres in production
5000 gallon yield

GRAPES GROWN:
Chardonnay
Gewurztraminer
Pinot Noir
Riesling

WINES PRODUCED:
Fox Run Sparkling Wine–*made from Pinot Noir and Chardonnay*
Chardonnay
Riesling
Ruby Vixen–*a blush made from Pinot Noir*
Special Reserve Riesling–*a dessert wine*

RECENT AWARDS: Have yet to enter competitions.

PRICING:
$5.99 to $10.99 per bottle, case discounts available.
MasterCard and Visa accepted.

AVAILABILITY: Throughout central New York.

TASTING AND TOURS:
Open May through October, Monday through Saturday, 10 AM to 5 PM; Sunday, noon to 5 PM.
Open November through April, Saturday, 10 AM to 5 PM; Sunday, noon to 5 PM, and by appointment.
$1.00 charge for tastings, refunded with purchase of Chardonnay or Riesling.
Tours not available.

AMBERG WINE CELLARS

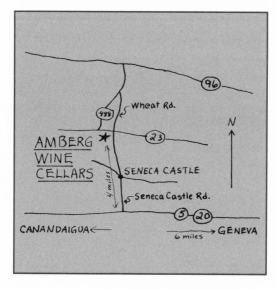

German-born Herman and Ute Amberg met when Herman returned to Germany for a visit in 1958. He came back to his job at the New York Agricultural Experiment Station and Ute joined him in the United States. They started a commercial grapevine nursery and in 1968 Herman left the Experiment Station to devote himself full-time to this business. Today, they sell their vines throughout the United States, predominantly along the eastern seaboard.

In 1984 the Ambergs purchased this 200-year-old farm. When their son Eric expressed an interest in winemaking, the Ambergs planted grapes and modernized the farm buildings. With studies in pomology (fruit science), degrees in enology (winemaking) and chemistry, and a year in Germany, Eric felt ready to open a winery. His mother Ute manages the tasting room as well as the ever-growing grapevine nursery business.

An old barn and shed have become a modern, light, high-ceilinged tasting room with space to accommodate many visitors. Ute envisions additional remodelling, including a stone courtyard. However, the Ambergs do not intend to expand production much. They hope to keep this a family-operated business and Eric prefers tending his winemaking responsibilities without help. And although Eric loves experimenting with new wines, Ute believes that offering more than their line of eight wines would diminish a visitor's wine-tasting experience.

This winery is off the beaten path of the other Seneca Lake wineries, but is only 10 miles from Geneva, and the Ambergs aim to offer wines which make the trip worthwhile.

AMBERG WINE CELLARS

2412 Seneca Castle Road, Clifton Springs, NY 14432
Phone: (315) 462-3455

OWNER: Herman Amberg

WINEMAKER: Eric Amberg

ESTABLISHED: Property purchased 1984
First planting 1985
First vintage 1989

PRODUCTION: 12 acres planted
10 acres in production
5,000 gallon yield
Grapes are sold.

GRAPES GROWN: Cabernet Sauvignon
Carmine
Chambourcin
Chardonnay
Muscat Ottonel
NY 65.533.13 (an as yet unnamed hybrid)
Pinot Noir
Riesling
Vidal

WINES PRODUCED: Chardonnay
Riesling
Courtyard Blanc–*a blend of Vidal and 65.533.13*
Courtyard Pearl–*a blend of 65.533.13 and Vidal*
Courtyard Gypsy–*a blend of 65.533.13 and Riesling*
Courtyard Blush–*a blend of Vidal, 65,533.13, Riesling, and Carmine*
Pinot Noir
Courtyard Burgundy–*a blend Pinot Noir, Cabernet Sauvignon, Cabernet Franc, Merlot, and Carmine*

RECENT AWARDS: Have yet to enter competitions.

PRICING: $5.99 to $11.99 per bottle; case discounts available.
MasterCard and Visa accepted.

AVAILABILITY: At selected restaurants and liquor stores in central New York.

TASTINGS AND TOURS: Open year round, Monday through Friday, 1 PM to 6 PM; Saturday, 10 AM to 6 PM; Sunday, noon to 6 PM.
No charge for tastings.
Tours available weekends.

NEW LAND VINEYARD

"Wine draws you in and takes you places," says Nancy Burdick. Pleasure in wine has taken Nancy from a job as a wine steward, to work at Heron Hill Vineyards, and now to managing her own winery with her husband Andrew. After years of searching for the perfect vineyard location, they've settled on this gentle hill above Seneca Lake.

It was Dr. Frank, the first successful planter of vinifera grapes in the Finger Lakes, who impressed the Burdicks with the potential of vinifera grapes in a carefully chosen location. This particular site is very well protected. Winter winds are warmed as they cross Seneca Lake on a long northwesterly diagonal path, so New Land's vines sustain less winter damage than those of many other vineyards. Isolation from other vineyards minimizes contamination by contagious vineyard diseases.

New Land is the only winery in the Finger Lakes to produce Sauvignon Blanc wines and the first to

grow Merlot grapes. Though the Burdicks were warned that these grapes were too delicate to survive here, they are flourishing. An example of their thorough and well-researched approach to grape growing is their Pinot Noir acreage, which actually includes thirteen different clones of Pinot Noir. Since each clone varies in a different way each year, the resulting mix insures a complex, superior wine every vintage.

A long driveway leads to the vineyards, winery, and tasting room. The Burdicks recently doubled the size of their winery. By digging the winery into the ground and berming up dirt on three sides, the winery maintains a fairly constant temperature, and any temperature change is gradual. This earth-buffered temperature control protects the wines year round.

Nancy and Andrew intend to grow no more than twelve acres of grapes, a quantity which they themselves can cultivate and harvest with minimal outside help. Focusing on the quality, not the quantity of wine production, they are setting out to prove that Finger Lakes wines can be truly great.

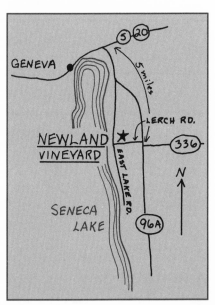

74

NEW LAND VINEYARD

577 Lerch Road, Geneva, NY 14456
Phone: (315) 585-9844

OWNERS:	Nancy and Andrew Burdick
WINEMAKERS:	Nancy and Andrew Burdick
ESTABLISHED:	Property purchased 1982 First planting 1982 First vintage 1987

PRODUCTION:

10 acres planted
10 acres in production
6,000 gallon yield
Grapes are neither purchased nor sold.

GRAPES GROWN:

Cabernet Sauvignon
Chardonnay
Gewurztraminer
Merlot
Pinot Noir
Riesling
Sauvignon Blanc

WINES PRODUCED:

Sauvignon Blanc
Chardonnay
Riesling
Gewurztraminer
Pinot Noir
Merlot
Cabernet Sauvignon
Late Harvest Sauvignon Blanc
Late Harvest Riesling

RECENT AWARDS: 1989 Chardonnay–*1991 Empire State Wine Classic, Gold Medal and Best Buy*
Rarely enter competitions.

PRICING: $7.00 to $15.00 per bottle; case discounts available.
MasterCard and Visa accepted.

AVAILABILITY: At selected restaurants and liquor stores in central New York.

TASTINGS AND TOURS:

Open May through October, daily, noon to 5 PM and by appointment.
$2.00 charge for tastings.
Limited tour available.

LAMOREAUX LANDING WINE CELLERS

Lamoreaux Landing was a steamboat landing from which local fruit was shipped to New York City and Rochester in the early 1900's. Although the old pilings are still here, this landing has become the grape-growing site for Lamoreaux Landing Wine Cellars, founded by Finger Lakes native Mark Wagner.

Mark is the owner of Wagner Farms which was established by his parents in 1949. Wagner Farms specializes in growing vinifera grapes. Lamoreaux Landing Wine Cellars is located on more recently acquired vineyard land which has been replanted with vinifera. A total of 140 acres of grapes are in production. All wines produced at Lamoreaux since 1991 are estate bottled.

Mark Wagner has worked closely with others to design a small, premium-quality winery with a production capacity of 7,000 gallons. The building, constructed in a modern rendition of Greek Revival style, enjoys a view spanning two-thirds of Seneca Lake. At this writing, the winery and its tasting room are in the final stages of construction and are about to be opened to the public.

Winemaker Rob Thomas joined his friend Mark at Lamoreaux Landing Wine Cellars in 1991, bringing with him extensive winemaking and vineyard experience. Rob and Mark intend to age wines well in the bottle and hold back wines until they are really ready to drink.

The starting lineup of Lamoreaux Landing wines, released in the summer of 1992, includes a 1990 Chardonnay, a 1990 Pinot Noir, a 1990 Red Table Wine, a 1991 Pinot Noir Blanc, a 1991 Semi-dry Riesling, a 1991 Dry Riesling, and a 1991 Gewürztraminer. Plans call for a later release of a 1990 sparkling wine and a Riesling ice wine.

1 9 9 1
ESTATE BOTTLED

LAMOREAUX
LANDING

FINGER LAKES

Gewürztraminer

ALC. 12.2% BY VOL. 750 ML

Winery Under Construction

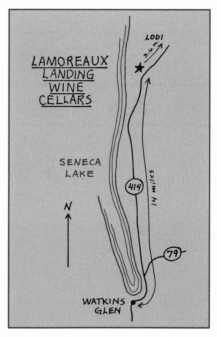

LAMOREAUX LANDING WINE CELLARS

SENECA LAKE

N

LODI

414

14 miles

79

WATKINS GLEN

LAMOREAUX LANDING WINE CELLERS

Route 414, Lodi, NY 14860
Phone: (607) 582-6011

OWNER: Mark Wagner

WINEMAKER: Robert Thomas

ESTABLISHED: Property owned by family since 1949
First planting 1890
First vintage 1990

PRODUCTION: 130 acres planted
125 acres in production
7000 gallon yield
Grapes are sold (eight varieties in addition to those listed below).

GRAPES GROWN: Cabernet Franc
Cabernet Sauvignon
Chardonnay
Gewurztraminer
Merlot
Pinot Noir
Riesling

WINES PRODUCED: Blanc de Blanc–*a sparkling wine made from Chardonnay*
Brut Sparkling Wine–*made from Pinot Noir and Chardonnay*
Blanc de Noir–*a sparkling wine made from Pinot Noir*
Chardonnay
Reserve Chardonnay
Riesling
Gewurztraminer
White Table Wine–*a changing blend*
Blush–*made from Pinot Noir*
Red Table Wine–*a blend of Pinot Noir and Cabernet Sauvignon*
Pinot Noir
Merlot
Riesling Ice Wine

RECENT AWARDS: Have yet to enter competitions.

PRICING: $6.00 to $15.00 per bottle, case discounts available.
MasterCard and Visa accepted.

AVAILABILITY: Wines available at winery after June 1992.

TASTINGS AND TOURS: Open year round, Monday through Saturday, 10 AM to 5 PM;
Sunday noon to 5 PM.
No charge for tastings.
Tours are available.

WAGNER VINEYARDS

Estate Bottled

WAGNER
Vineyards

1990
Finger Lakes
Gewürztraminer

An Aromatic Semi-Dry Wine

PRODUCED & BOTTLED BY WAGNER VINEYARDS, LODI, N.Y.
ALC. 10.4% BY VOLUME   750 ML.

CONTAINS SULFITES

Bill Wagner has been farming grapes in the Finger Lakes since 1947 and has seen a lot of changes over the years. Originally a contract grape grower for the large wineries, as well as a dairy and food crop farmer, Bill switched entirely to grapes in the 1960's. Today he uses almost half of his crop in his own wines. His modern octagonal-shaped winery, well-organized tours and tastings, effective product distribution, and many awards attest to Bill's serious dedication to winemaking.

Bill considers the winery an ongoing experiment. He and his winemakers are always learning and making changes to produce better grapes and wines. Even with these changes, Wagner wines have a distinctive, readily recognizable style, earning critical acclaim.

At this large and popular winery, guided tours are offered regularly, followed by a selective tasting of many wines. After the organized tasting, additional wines can be sampled for a modest price. The extensive line of wines includes those of native American grapes, European vinifera, and many French-American hybrids. At Wagner Vineyards it is possible to taste and contrast four different styles of Riesling, sample barrel-fermented white wines, and try a number of well-made labrusca wines.

Wagner's Ginny Lee Cafe, next door, has exchanged its large tent for a permanent structure and is now open year-round. The spacious interior seats 220 and the wraparound porch can accommodate 100. Special wine matching dinners and other events held at the cafe are announced in the winery's newsletter. The cafe is available for wedding receptions, banquets, and parties. Guests may enjoy wine, food, and a spectacular view of Seneca Lake.

WAGNER VINEYARDS

Route 414, Lodi, NY 14860
Phone: (607) 582-6450
Cafe: (607) 582-6574

OWNER: Bill Wagner

WINEMAKERS: John Herbert and Ann Raffetto

ESTABLISHED:
Property purchased 1947
First planting 1947
First vintage 1978

PRODUCTION:
220 acres planted
200 acres in production
60,000 gallon yield
Grapes are sold.

GRAPES GROWN:

Aurore	Melody
Cabernet Franc	Merlot
Cabernet Sauvignon	Niagara
Cayuga	Pinot Noir
Chardonnay	Riesling
DeChaunac	Seyval
Delaware	Vidal
Gewurztraminer	Vignoles

WINES PRODUCED:

Reserve White–*a blend of Seyval, Vidal, and Cayuga*
Chardonnay
Reserve Chardonnay
Chardonnay LaMoreaux Vineyard
Seyval Blanc (barrel fermented)
Gewurztraminer
Johannisberg Riesling–*fermented dry*
Johannisberg Riesling (semi-sweet)
Melody–*a recent hybrid*
Wagner's Seyval
Alta Blanc–*a blend of Vidal, Cayuga, and Seyval*
Ravat Blanc
Delaware
Niagara
Manhattan Blush–*a changing blend of French-American varieties*
Pinot Noir Blanc
Alta Blush–*a changing blend of French-American varieties*
Reserve Blush–*a changing blend*
Rose–*a changing blend of French-American varieties*
Vintner's Noir–*a blend of Pinot Noir and Rougeon*
Pinot Noir
Reserve Red–*a blend of DeChaunac, Rougeon, and Pinot Noir*
DeChaunac
Alta B–*a semi-sweet blend of DeChaunac and Rougeon*
Johannisberg Riesling–*Late Harvest*
Vidal Ice Wine
Johannisberg Riesling Ice Wine
Ravat Ice Wine
Port
Blush Grape Juice–*a non-alcoholic blend of Cayuga, Vignoles, and Rougeon*
Johannisberg Riesling Grape Juice
Ravat Juice

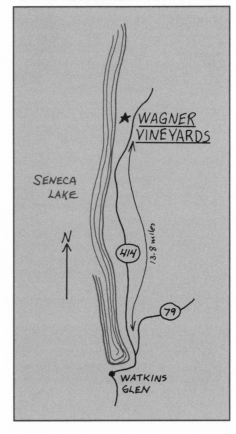

RECENT AWARDS: 1990 Gewurztraminer–*1991 Les Amis du Vin, Silver Medal*
1989 Johannisberg Riesling Ice Wine–*1991 LADV, Gold Medal; 1991 New York State Fair, Gold Medal; 1991International Eastern Wine Competition, Bronze Medal*
1989 Ravat Ice Wine–*1991 Tasters' Guild, Gold Medal*
1989 Johannisberg Riesling–*1991 Los Angeles County Fair, Gold Medal*
1988 Gewurztraminer–*1991 Dallas Morning News, Silver Medal; LADV, Silver Medal*
1988 Barrel Fermented Seyval Blanc–*1991 LADV, Silver Medal; 1991 IEWC, Silver Medal; 1991 NYSF, Bronze Medal; 1991 TG, Silver Medal*
Many other awards consistently received.

PRICING: $3 to $18 per bottle; case discounts available.
MasterCard and Visa accepted.

AVAILABILITY: Available throughout New York State, and in Colorado, Maryland, New Jersey, Washington D.C., Chicago, San Francisco, Toronto, and London.

TASTINGS AND TOURS:

Open all year, Monday through Friday, 10 AM to 4:30 PM; Saturday and Sunday, 10 AM to 5 PM.
Closed Thanksgiving, Christmas, and New Year's Day.
No charge for tastings.
Guided tours daily.
Ginny Lee Cafe open for lunch, dinner and Sunday brunch; call ahead for service hours, (607) 582-6574.

POPLAR RIDGE VINEYARDS

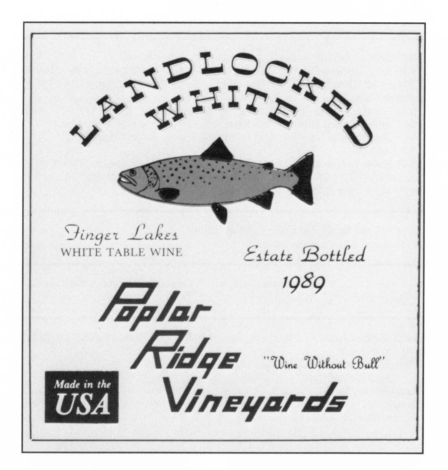

LANDLOCKED WHITE

Finger Lakes
WHITE TABLE WINE

Estate Bottled 1989

Poplar Ridge Vineyards

"*Wine Without Bull*"

Made in the USA

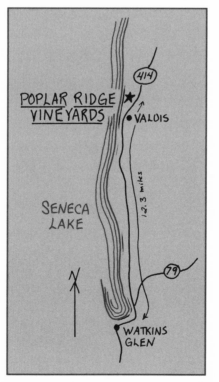

POPLAR RIDGE VINEYARDS

• VALOIS

414

SENECA LAKE

12.3 miles

79

WATKINS GLEN

Every day while working at Wagner Vineyards, Dave Bagley drove past the present home of Poplar Ridge Vineyards and said, "I have to have that property!" Eventually, he did purchase it, and now, after years of making wine for others, he's on his own.

Big letters on both winery and wine labels proclaim Dave's motto: "Wine Without Bull." Dave feels that it is the winemaker's obligation to make a clean, balanced, sound wine. To do this, he says, one must use good grapes "and don't monkey around with them." He admires the Gallo Winery in California, feeling that their wines are very clean, and seeks to emulate their style. Dave believes that the wine is started in the vineyard and he strives to grow the grapes well and to harvest at just the right time. He finishes the wine, not in a laboratory, but in the wineglass. He decides on sweetness levels, acid, balance and such by taste, not by scientific analysis in the lab.

This winery is built, as Dave puts it, on Yankee ingenuity. He built the winery himself, designed and built some of the equipment, and maintains and repairs all of it. An assertive, thoughtful, political person, Dave feels that the main profit of the wine business is in the lifestyle. He finds a sense of accomplishment in looking over the vineyards. However, he's concerned about the current political and economic climate and hopes to survive what he calls the "anti-alcohol witch hunt."

With hunting and fishing mementoes on the walls, the tasting room reflects Dave's love of the outdoors. Picture windows overlook Seneca Lake, and visitors can enjoy the view and friendly atmosphere as they sample the many wines available for tasting.

POPLAR RIDGE VINEYARDS

Route 414, Valois, NY 14888
Phone: (607) 582-6421

OWNER:	Dave Bagley
WINEMAKER:	Dave Bagley
ESTABLISHED:	Property purchased 1977 First planting 1979 First vintage 1981
PRODUCTION:	26 acres planted 26 acres in production 15,000 gallon yield Some grapes are purchased; juice is sold.
GRAPES GROWN:	Cabernet Sauvignon Carmine Cayuga Chardonnay Chelois Merlot Riesling Sauvignon Blanc Seyval Vidal Vignoles
WINES PRODUCED:	Champagne–*a changing blend* Landlocked White–*a blend of Seyval and Cayuga* Johannisberg Riesling Cayuga White Vidal Blanc Ravat Brittany's Blush–*a blend of Seyval, Cayuga, and Chelois* Catawba Pink Valois Rouge–*100% Chelois* Baco Noir Dave's Big Red–*a blend of Cabernet Sauvignon and Carmine*
RECENT AWARDS:	Numerous awards consistently received.
PRICING:	$5.00 to $10.00 per bottle; case discounts available. MasterCard and Visa accepted.
AVAILABILITY:	At a few local restaurants and liquor stores. Will ship UPS throughout New York.
TASTINGS AND TOURS:	Open May through October, Monday through Saturday, 10 AM to 5 PM; Sunday, noon to 5 PM. Open November through April, Saturday and Sunday, noon to 5 PM. No charge for tastings. Informal tour available.

HAZLITT 1852 VINEYARDS

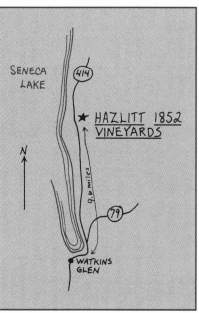

The Hazlitt family knows grapes; they've been grape farming this land since 1852. Jerry Hazlitt has grown grapes all his life and has always made wines for his own table. When the wholesale market for grapes declined, the Hazlitts were ready to open their own winery.

Tastings are held in a charming barn decorated with Indian artifacts and old farm implements. At a curved wooden bar, a member of the family often hosts tastings. A popcorn maker graces one counter. The Hazlitts have created a casual, friendly atmosphere and they enjoy sharing their time with visitors.

Jerry stays involved, although son Phil does most of the winemaking. Son Doug captains schooner cruises which leave two or three times daily from the winery. Call ahead for reservations.

The back half of the barn houses the winery, which is filled with moderate-sized stainless steel tanks. In their winemaking the Hazlitts strive for clean, well-balanced, fruity wines. They utilize many native American grapes as well as hybrids and European vinifera. This is a family operation, and they don't want to produce more wine than they can make and distribute themselves. However, they get busier each year and have grown fivefold in six years to keep up with demand. They still sell out all of their wines every year and take great satisfaction in pleasing their customers.

HAZLITT 1852 VINEYARDS

Route 414, Hector, NY 14841
Phone: (607) 546-5812

OWNERS: Jerry and Elaine Hazlitt

WINEMAKERS: Phil and Jerry Hazlitt

ESTABLISHED:
Property purchased 1852
First planting 1852
First vintage 1984

PRODUCTION:
45 acres planted
42 acres in production
15,000 gallon yield
Some grapes are purchased; grapes are sold.

GRAPES GROWN:

L'Ambertille (SV23-512)	Concord
Aurore	Gewurztraminer
Cabernet Sauvignon	Merlot
Catawba	Riesling
Cayuga	Seyval
Chardonnay	Vidal

WINES PRODUCED:
Chardonnay
Johannisberg Riesling
L'Ambertille–*made from a French hybrid grown in New York only by the Hazlitts*
Schooner White–*a blend of Cayuga, Vidal, and Seyval*
Vidal Blanc
Cayuga White
Aurore
White Stag–*a blend of Vidal, Aurore, and Cayuga*
Seyval Blanc
Ravat-51
Diamond Rose
Cabin Fever–*made from Catawba*
Red Cat–*a blend of Catawba and Baco Noir*
Baco Noir
Schooner Red–*a blend of Pinot Noir and Baco Noir*
Pinot Noir

RECENT AWARDS:
1990 Ravat-51–*1991 International Eastern Wine Competition, Bronze Medal*
1989 Chardonnay–*1990 IEWC, Silver Medal*
1989 Johannisberg Riesling–*1990 IEWC, Bronze Medal*

PRICING:
$5.00 to $11.00 per bottle; case discounts available.
MasterCard and Visa accepted.

AVAILABILITY: In central New York restaurants and liquor stores.

TASTINGS AND TOURS:
Open April through December, Monday through Saturday, 10 AM to 6 PM;
  Sunday, noon to 6 PM.
Open January through March, Friday, Saturday, and Sunday, noon to 5 PM.
No charge for tastings.
Tours are not available.

CHATEAU LaFAYETTE RENEAU

Dick and Betty Reno fell in love with the Finger Lakes when driving through the area. While still living in Massachusetts, they purchased a sixty-three acre farm plus nearly fifty adjoining acres, began replanting the old vineyards, and hired a winemaker. They immediately began producing wines, purchasing all grapes until their own vines matured. Visiting weekends from New England, the Renos oversaw the renovation, equipping, and expansion of the winery. They have now settled in the completely refurbished brick house in front of the winery.

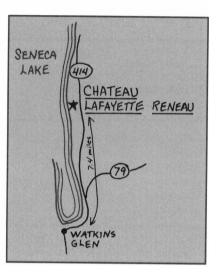

Now growing all of the grapes they use, the Renos look forward to the time when the entire vineyard will come into production. Dave Whiting, the new winemaker, is excited by the winery's movement towards red wines. 1991 marked the winery's first nouveau-style wine. Additionally, Cabernet Sauvignon vines have been planted as well as more Pinot Noir. A barrel-fermented Seyval-Chardonnay blend has been added to the winery's lineup, as well as a late harvest Riesling.

The tasting room and winery are set in a beautifully renovated nineteenth-century barn, where a changing array of antiques is displayed. The very large wine barrel attached to the front of the winery actually houses the circular stairs leading to the cellar where the wine is made. The tour of this well-appointed winery can be as brief or as detailed as visitors wish.

Throughout the summer, Chateau LaFayette Reneau offers hayrides through the vineyard. Samples of wine made from each grape variety are offered as visitors reach the corresponding section of the vineyard. The hayride is followed by a buffet dinner. Call ahead for the hayride schedule.

Two ponds and the landscaped vineyards enhance the wonderful view over Seneca Lake. Visitors may enjoy the scene from the large deck, where they are welcome to bring a picnic lunch. Feeding the ducks provides a pleasant diversion for children.

CHATEAU LaFAYETTE RENEAU

Route 414, Hector, NY 14841
Phone: (607) 546-2062

OWNERS: Dick and Betty Reno

WINEMAKER: David Whiting

ESTABLISHED:
Property purchased 1985
First planting 1986
First vintage 1985

PRODUCTION:
35 acres planted
22 acres in production
12,000 gallon yield
Grapes are neither purchased nor sold.

GRAPES GROWN:

Cabernet Sauvignon	Pinot Noir
Catawba	Riesling
Chardonnay	Seyval
Niagara	

WINES PRODUCED:
Chardonnay
Johannisberg Riesling
Seyval-Chardonnay
Seyval
Cuvée Blanc–*a blend of Riesling and Seyval*
Pinot Noir Blanc–*a blush wine*
Niagara Mist
Meadow Mist–*a rosé wine blending Catawba, Baco Noir, and Seyval*
Cuvée Rouge–*made from Pinot Noir*
Nouveau–*made from Pinot Noir*
Pinot Noir
Select Late Harvest Riesling

RECENT AWARDS:
NV Seyval-Chardonnay–*1992 Tasters Guild International, Silver Medal*
1991 Pinot Noir Blanc–*1992 TGI, Bronze Medal; 1992 San Diego National Wine Competition, Bronze Medal*
1991 Meadow Mist–*1992 International Eastern Wine Competition, Silver Medal*
1989 Riesling–*1991 New York State Fair, Bronze Medal; 1991 IEWC, Bronze Medal; 1992 TGI, Silver Medal, 1992 SDNWC, Silver Medal*
1989 Chardonnay–*1991 NYSF, Bronze Medal*

PRICING:
$4.49 to $10.99 per bottle; case discounts available.
MasterCard, Visa and American Express accepted. $25 minimum purchase on American Express.

AVAILABILITY: At selected restaurants and liquor stores in New York State.

TASTINGS AND TOURS:
Open March through October, Monday through Saturday, 10 AM to 6 PM; Sunday, noon to 6 PM.
Open November and December, Saturday noon to 5 PM; Sunday noon to 4 PM.
Open January and February by appointment.
$1.00 charge to taste up to three wines; $2.50 charge to taste all the wines, souvenir glass included.
Informal tours, as simple or detailed as desired.
Bus tours welcome by appointment.

ROLLING VINEYARDS

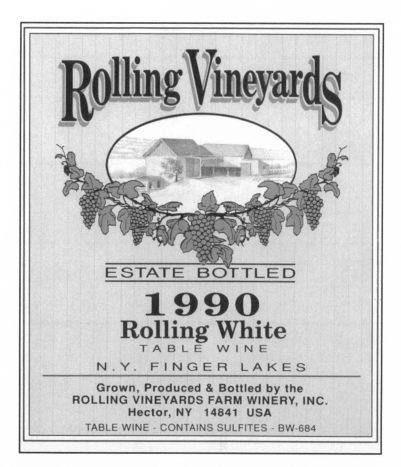

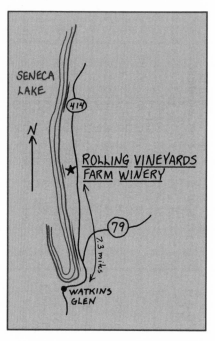

Hailing from the Rochester area, Ed Grow spent his summers in the Finger Lakes, where he met many grape growers and winemakers. The Grow family, thinking they would enjoy running their own grape and winery operation in a country setting, entered the business prudently–purchasing their farm in 1977, planting additional grapes a year later, upgrading the buildings, and waiting until 1981 to make their first vintage.

The Grows sell most of their grapes to other wineries. Ed is known locally for growing good, healthy grapes. He says his hillside's southwestern exposure allows the fruit to mature well, resulting in excellent sugar levels and a delicious fruitiness. The Grows would like to plant even more grapes, including new vinifera varieties, and have recently planted more Chardonnay. They have significantly expanded production and may build additional cellaring space and add on to the tasting room. However, they will expand cautiously and avoid overextending themselves.

The tasting room is a cool, panelled room with windows overlooking Seneca Lake. Tee shirts, baskets, and wine-related items are available for purchase. Rolling Vineyards is located right next door to Chateau LaFayette Reneau, and the two wineries share a panoramic view of several ponds, seemingly landscaped vineyards, and Seneca Lake. Outdoor picnic tables afford a view over the cascading vineyards and the lake.

ROLLING VINEYARDS

5055 Route 414, Hector, NY 14841
Phone: (607) 546-9302

OWNERS: Ed and JoAnne Grow

WINEMAKER: Ed Grow

ESTABLISHED:
Property purchased 1977
First planting 1978
First vintage 1981

PRODUCTION:

50 acres planted
50 acres in production
8,000 gallon yield
Grapes are sold.

GRAPES GROWN:

Cayuga	Pinot Noir
Chancellor	Riesling
Chardonnay	Seyva
Chelois	Vidal
Gewurztraminer	Vignoles
Marechal Foch	Villard

WINES PRODUCED:

Chardonnay
Gewurztraminer
Johannisberg Riesling
Cayuga White
Seyval
Vidal
Rolling White–*a changing blend*
Lady's Blush–*a changing blend*
Rolling Red–*a changing blend*
Chelois
Marechal Foch
Chancellor
Pinot Noir
Vignoles–*a dessert wine*

RECENT AWARDS:
1990 Seyval–*1991 New York State Fair, Bronze Medal*
1989 Vidal–*1991 New York Wine & Food Classic, Bronze Medal*
1988 Chardonnay–*1991 NYW&FC, Bronze Medal*

PRICING:
$5.00 to $10.00 per bottle; case discounts available.
MasterCard and Visa accepted, $15.00 minimum.

AVAILABILITY:
Available throughout New York State, except in New York City.
Will ship UPS throughout New York.

TASTINGS AND TOURS:

Open May through October, Monday through Saturday, 10 AM to 5 PM;
  Sunday, noon to 5 PM.
Open November through Christmas, and in April, Saturday, 10 AM to 5 PM;
  Sunday, noon to 5 PM.
No charge for tastings.
Tours available on request.

WINE TASTING

Tasting wine can be a pleasurable and rewarding pursuit; here are a few tips to help you get the most pleasure and knowledge out of your experience. Just remember, it's your own taste you are looking to please.

Most wineries offer several wines for tasting. Wines will usually be poured from driest to sweetest, beginning with white, then blush, red, and finally dessert wines. You are encouraged to take tasting notes to help you record your responses to each wine.

At the winery your host will pour just a small amount of wine in a glass. A few sips are all you need to examine a wine. If you don't want to finish the glass, feel free to pour out the excess in a "dump bucket." The point is to taste wines, not to imbibe so much that your taste buds become muddled. Some wineries offer various foods to accompany tastings or sell various snacks. Bland foods such as crackers may cleanse the palate, while stronger foods such as cheese and meats may complement a wine and demonstrate how well it would accompany a meal.

Drinking wine involves four of the five senses–sight, smell, taste, and touch. (Perhaps people clink glasses to include the fifth sense, hearing.) First, take a look at the wine. Hold the glass up to the light and examine its color and clarity. How does it compare with other wines made of the same grape? Gently swirl the wine in the glass to release the

wine's bouquet or aroma. Smell the wine. What do you detect? Is it fragrant and fruity, oaky, attractive, unpleasant? What does it tell you about the wine? If the nose seems limited, give it a minute and swirl it again.

Now taste the wine. Take a small sip to run through all parts of your mouth. How does it register on different parts of your tongue? How sweet is it? Is the sugar well balanced by acid? If you taste oak, does it marry well with the wine? Note the tannin level in red wines. Tannin is that astringent acid–also present in tea–which prolongs the life of the wine, adds to the robust-

ness, and softens with age. Does its piquancy add to the wine, or is it an unpleasant obstacle?

Professional judges will spit rather than swallow, but the winery experience is not a rigorous one, and you won't find people spitting wines here. So swallow the wine. Consider the finish or aftertaste. Does it linger or is it short? Are there any new characteristics introduced?

Take another sip. Is it different from the first? In what ways? As the wine breathes or is exposed to air, more of its taste and nose are released. After a certain point, exposure to air will cause the wine to become oxidized and deteriorate. Consider how the wine might accompany a meal. Can it stand up to heartier foods, or does it require something more delicate? Or is it a sipping wine to be enjoyed by itself?

Take home a few bottles of the wines you enjoyed, and cellar them if you feel they'll benefit from additional bottle ageing. Drink them at leisure. Take notice of the difference between drinking a glass of wine and your tasting at the winery. You'll find that over time your tastes may change as you become better able to detect and enjoy additional nuances in wine. All this comes with experience. In wine tasting there are no right answers. The real criterion is whether *you* like it.

CAYUGA LAKE WINERIES

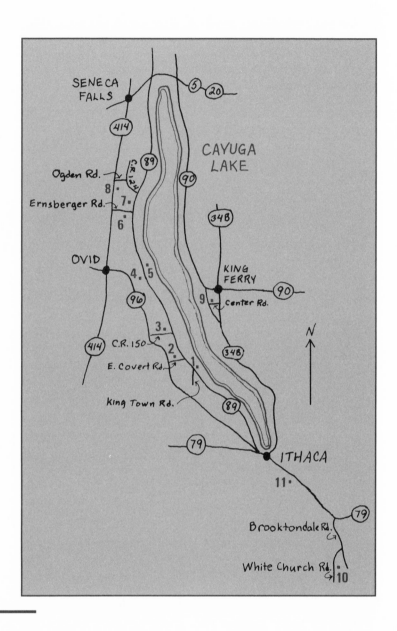

FRONTENAC POINT VINEYARD

Jim Doolittle knows the Finger Lakes area well. An Elmira native, he attended Cornell University, earned a degree in economics, and pursued graduate studies in viticulture. As a marketing specialist for the State Department of Agriculture, he specialized in grapes and wine, his work culminating in writing the Farm Winery Bill of 1976.

Once passed, this Act permitted a farm winery to retail its own wine, making the small winery economically feasible. Carol Doolittle, also employed by the Agriculture Department, started the annual wine judging at the New York State Fair.

In 1977, the Doolittles decided to buy a farm to grow grapes and make wine themselves. Their research revealed Ithaca, New York, as the city with the highest wine consumption per capita in the nation at that time. With Ithaca as their intended market, they bought land and planted grapes on the western shore of Cayuga Lake, just 12 miles north of Ithaca. The first year they commuted from their home near Albany to tend the vines. They built a house on their new farm, settled in, and devoted themselves to the winery. Carol, never one to sit still, also works full time at Cornell University, marketing cooperative extension publications.

Jim recently erected a new wine-making building with a tasting room. Previously the winery had not been open to the public, but Jim chose to open a tasting room because of the changing wholesale market and increasing prohibitionist pressures. He intends to use the tasting room as an information center on the health benefits of moderate wine consumption.

Jim characterizes his wines as French in style. They are dry, well-oaked, and include several award-winning red wines. After years of experimentation, he is pleased with his grape varieties, choice of wines, and his new contact with satisfied customers.

Frontenac Point Vineyard
1988
Seyval

FINGER LAKES TABLE WINE
Produced and Bottled by
Frontenac Point Vineyard
Rte. 89, Trumansburg, NY

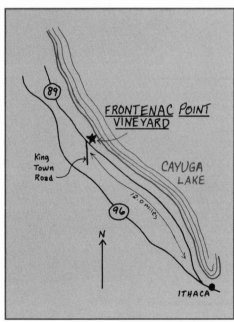

FRONTENAC POINT VINEYARD

RD 3, Box 112, Route 89, Trumansburg, NY 14886
Phone: (607) 387-9619

OWNERS: Jim and Carol Doolittle

WINEMAKER: Jim Doolittle

ESTABLISHED:
Property purchased 1978
First planting 1978
First vintage 1982

PRODUCTION:
24 acres planted
24 acres in production
6,000 gallon yield
Grapes are sold.

GRAPES GROWN:
Chambourcin
Chardonnay
Chelois
Marechal Foch
Muscat Ottonel
Pinot Noir
Riesling
Seyval
Vidal
Vignoles

WINES PRODUCED:
Chardonnay
Dry Riesling
Blanc de Blanc Reserve–*a blend of Vidal and Riesling*
Seyval
Chateau Doolittle–*Blanc de Noir made from Chambourcin*
Nouveau Red–*a blend of Marechal Foch and Pinot Noir*
Proprietor's Reserve–*a blend of Chelois, Chambourcin, and Pinot Noir*
Chambourcin
Late Harvest Vignoles–*includes some Muscat Ottonel*

RECENT AWARDS: No longer enter competitions.

PRICING: $5.50 to $12.00 per bottle; case discounts available.

AVAILABILITY: Widely available at liquor stores and restaurants in Ithaca; limited availability in Binghamton, Syracuse, and Albany.

TASTINGS AND TOURS:
Open May through December, Thursday through Sunday, 10 AM to 4 PM, and by appointment.
No charge for tastings.
Limited tours upon request.

AMERICANA VINEYARDS

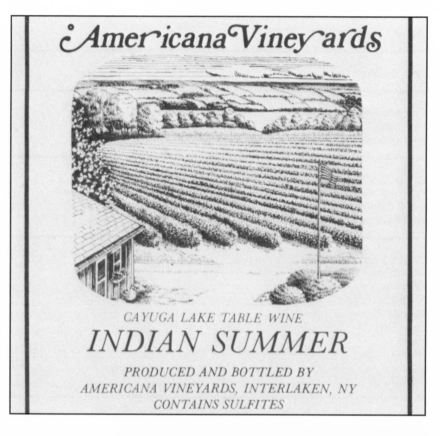

Americana Vineyards

CAYUGA LAKE TABLE WINE

INDIAN SUMMER

PRODUCED AND BOTTLED BY
AMERICANA VINEYARDS, INTERLAKEN, NY
CONTAINS SULFITES

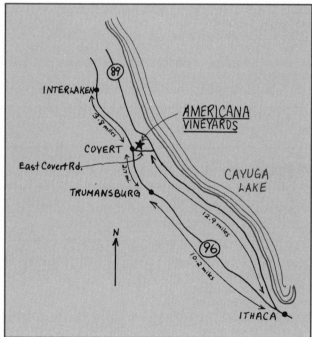

Jim Treble has been an avid home winemaker since he was a graduate student at Syracuse University over thirty years ago. Now a professor of communications at Ithaca College, he took the opportunity of his move to Ithaca in 1971 to settle on land suitable for grape growing. When he began making more wine than family and friends could possibly consume, acquaintances encouraged the Trebles to open their own winery.

Jim and Mary Anne Treble have converted their four-car shop into a winery and cozy tasting room with a wood stove and colonial decor. Their winery, well-outfitted with small scale equipment, is an interesting contrast to larger wineries. As tour guides, Mary Anne and daughter Allison lead visitors into the winemaking area just behind the tasting room and explain the winemaking process and thoroughly answer visitors' questions. At the tour's finish, a visitor may personally cork a wine bottle.

Americana wines are available only at the winery; the Trebles sell all of their wine each year and have increased production to keep up with demand. They intend to remain a small, family-run winery, and take pride in having achieved their goals.

AMERICANA VINEYARDS

4367 East Covert Road, Interlaken, NY 14847
Phone: (607) 387-6801

OWNERS:	James and Mary Anne Treble
WINEMAKER:	James Treble
ESTABLISHED:	Property purchased 1972 First planting 1973 First vintage 1981
PRODUCTION:	10 acres planted 10 acres in production 4,000 gallon yield Some grapes are purchased.
GRAPES GROWN:	Aurore Baco Noir Catawba Cayuga White Concord Marechal Foch Niagara Seyval Various vinifera plantings
WINES PRODUCED:	Riesling Cayuga White Seyval Aurore Niagara Indian Summer–*a blend of Catawba and DeChaunac* Vintners Nouveau–*made from Marechal Foch* Beefsteak–*made from Baco Noir* November Harvest–*a blend of all post-frost grapes*
RECENT AWARDS:	Do not enter competitions.
PRICING:	$4.75 to $7.95 per bottle; case discounts available. MasterCard and Visa accepted.
AVAILABILITY:	Only at the winery.

TASTINGS AND TOURS:	Open May through October, Monday through Saturday, 10 AM to 5 PM;
	  Sunday, noon to 5 PM.
	Open November through April, Saturday, 10 AM to 5 PM; Sunday, noon to 5 PM;
	  weekdays by appointment.
	No charge for tastings.
	Informal tour upon request; last tour 4:00 PM.

Bronx born, the Lucases followed their dreams to the Finger Lakes. Bill's boyhood summers on a farm gave him a taste for the pleasures of country life, leading him and his wife to purchase an Interlaken dairy farm. Turning the land over to vineyards, they sold their grapes for several years before opening the winery.

The original tasting room has a large picture window overlooking the vineyards and the shores of Cayuga Lake. Tastings are also offered in the adjoining winemaking room among the wine tanks and barrels. A corner of this room has been set aside for a display of wine related items available for purchase.

Ties to their former city life remain: the Tug Boat series of blended wines commemorates Bill's work as a tug boat captain in and around New York Harbor. This series includes Tug Boat White, Tug Boat Red, The Captain's Belle, and Evening Tide. Additionally, their club offering discounts on case purchases is called the Captain's Table Wine Club.

Sparkling wine is their latest venture. Steve DiFrancesco, the new winemaker, has a specialized background in champagne-making and is experimenting with classic champagne blends.

The winery has significantly increased production and Ruth Lucas is quite optimistic about the future. She feels that they have found their niche in the market and will do well with sparkling wines. Above all, the people at Lucas Vineyards focus on maintaining quality and aim to continue making award-winning wines.

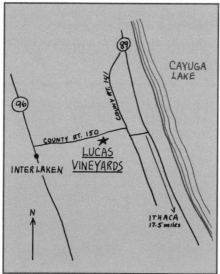

LUCAS VINEYARDS

County Road 150, Interlaken, NY 14847
Phone: (607) 532-4825

OWNERS:	William and Ruth Lucas
WINEMAKER:	Steve DiFrancesco
ESTABLISHED:	Property purchased 1974 First planting 1975 First vintage 1980
PRODUCTION:	21 acres planted 20 acres in production 17,000 gallon yield Grapes are sold.

GRAPES GROWN:

Cayuga	Rayon d'Or
Chardonnay	Riesling
DeChaunac	Seyval
Gewurztraminer	Vidal
Pinot Noir	Vignoles

WINES PRODUCED:

Champagne "Extra Dry"–*a proprietary blend*
Chardonnay
Private Reserve Chardonnay
Riesling
Gewurztraminer
Seyval Blanc
Cayuga White
Evening Tide–*a blend of Cayuga and Riesling*
Tug Boat White–*a blend of Cayuga and Vignoles*
The Captain's Belle–*a blush wine blending Cayuga, DeChaunac and Rayon d'Or*
Tug Boat Red–*a blend of Chancellor and DeChaunac*
Vignoles–*a dessert wine*

RECENT AWARDS:

1990 Cayuga–*1991 New York State Fair, Bronze Medal*
1990 Riesling–*1991 NYSF, Bronze Medal; 1991 Dallas Morning News World
    Wine Festival, Bronze Medal; 1992 San Diego National Wine Competition,
    Silver Medal*
1989 Champagne–*1991 NYSF, Silver Medal; 1992 SDNWC, Bronze Medal*
NV Tugboat White–*1991 DMNWWF, Bronze Medal; SDNWC, Silver Medal*
NV Evening Tide–*1991 NYSF, Bronze Medal*

PRICING:

$5.00 to $10.50 per bottle; quantity discounts available.
MasterCard, Visa and Discover accepted.

AVAILABILITY:

At restaurants and liquor stores throughout central New York.

TASTINGS AND TOURS:

Open Memorial Day weekend through October, Monday through Saturday,
    11 AM to 5 PM; Sunday, noon to 5 PM.
Open April through Memorial Day, and November through mid-December,
    Saturday, 11 AM to 5 PM; Sunday, noon to 5 PM.
$2.00 charge for tastings and souvenir glass.
Inquire about self-guided winery tour.

HOSMER

The Hosmer family, originally from Chicago, bought this lakeside farm in the 1930's for a summer home. In 1972, Cameron's father decided to plant grapes, and Cameron, while working at the farm, studied pomology (the science of fruit growing) at Cornell University.

Cameron and Maren made so much wine for friends and family that they decided to open a winery. To accommodate an increasing number of visitors, they recently built a new winery and tasting room by renovating an old barn across the road from their original retail space. The new tasting room, with a balcony for gift items and local information, is high-ceilinged, spacious, and light. The Hosmers offer a friendly place to visit and aim to put people at ease.

The Hosmers grow all their own grapes and enjoy controlling the winemaking process from vineyard through bottling. They work towards growing excellent fruit and enjoy the challenge of fulfilling the grapes' potential. Many wineries that purchase their grapes yield award-winning wines. They have doubled their own production in two years and intend continuing expansion. Cameron has recently replaced some vines, planting red wine grapes and more Chardonnay. Offering a range of wines from dry to semi-sweet, Hosmer has focused on drier white wines that go well with food. They also recently released two red vinifera wines. As he accumulates experience, Cameron concentrates on producing public pleasing wines and expects Hosmer wines to get better with each vintage.

Besides the Cayuga Wine Trail events, Hosmer features an annual Asparagus Day in early June, at which newly released Hosmer wines are matched with different preparations of this first vegetable of the year. Call ahead for details.

Semi-Dry

HOSMER

1990
SEYVAL

CAYUGA LAKE   NEW YORK

TABLE WINE PRODUCED & BOTTLED BY HOSMER, OVID, NY 14521
CONTAINS SULFITES

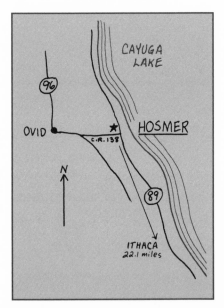

HOSMER

6999 Route 89, Ovid, NY 14521
Phone: (607) 869-5585

OWNERS: Cameron and Maren Hosmer

WINEMAKER: Cameron Hosmer

ESTABLISHED:
Property purchased 1930's
First planting 1972
First vintage 1985

PRODUCTION:
40 acres planted
40 acres in production
10,000 gallon yield
Grapes are sold.

GRAPES GROWN:
Cabernet Franc
Catawba
Cayuga
Chardonnay
DeChaunac
Pinot Noir
Riesling
Seyval

WINES PRODUCED:
Chardonnay
Riesling
Alpine–*a blend of Seyval and Chardonnay*
Seyval
Cayuga
Après–*a secret blend*
Pinot Noir
Cabernet Franc
Late Harvest Riesling

RECENT AWARDS:
1990 Riesling–*1991 New York State Fair, Bronze Medal*
1990 Cayuga–*1991 NYSF, Bronze Medal*
1989 Chardonnay–*1991 NYSF, Bronze Medal*
1989 Seyval–*1991 NYSF, Bronze Medal*

PRICING:
$5.00 to $10.00 per bottle.
MasterCard and Visa accepted.

AVAILABILITY: At restaurants and liquor stores throughout New York State.

TASTINGS AND TOURS:
Open April through December, Monday through Saturday, 10 AM to 5 PM;
  Sunday, noon to 5 PM.
Open January through March by appointment.
$2.00 charge for tastings and souvenir wine glass.
Tours are not available.

CAYUGA RIDGE ESTATE VINEYARD

In 1991, Susie and Tom Challen became co-owners of this well-respected Cayuga Lake winery. Formerly Plane's Cayuga Vineyard, it was established by Bob and Mary Plane in 1980 as an estate winery after a few years of contract grape growing. In the decade the Planes operated their winery, they were an influential presence in the local wine industry. Mary Plane is credited with founding the Cayuga Wine Trail.

The Challens come from Ontario, Canada. Tom worked there for 18 years in vineyard and wine research and as a winemaker. Originally contacting the Planes about a winemaking position, Tom told them to notify him if they ever wanted to sell the winery. A year later they did. Upon completion of a complex purchase agreement in 1990, Tom became general manager, gradually taking on ownership.

The Challens were willing to pick up their roots and relocate here because they feel this is such a fine winery. Tom believes the vineyards are in good shape with a fine mix of grapes, and the winemaking facilities are excellent. He intends to continue producing the varieties and style of wines the Planes did, with minor adjustments. The winery name has been changed to "reflect the viticultural region." The quatrefoil logo, a medieval symbol of quality, remains from the Plane's wine labels. Long-time customers continue to visit and have been pleased with the sense of continuity they find.

The Challens intend carrying on Bob and Mary's educational ideas. Tom has revived the Planes' vigneron program in which participants lease vines and can attend training sessions in vine management. The participants may harvest and use their grapes, or the winery will make it into wine for them for a fee. Grape juice and expert coaching are available to home winemakers each fall. Additionally, wine tasting seminars are offered in July. Call the winery for details.

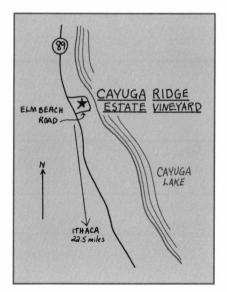

CAYUGA RIDGE ESTATE VINEYARD

6800 Route 89, Elm Beach Road, Ovid, NY 14521
Phone: (607) 869-5158

OWNERS: The Challen family

WINEMAKER: Tom Challen

ESTABLISHED:
Property originally purchased 1964
Purchased by current owners 1991
First planting 1972
First vintage 1980

PRODUCTION:

34 acres planted
34 acres in production
25,000 gallon yield
Grapes and juice are sold.

GRAPES GROWN:

Cayuga White
Chancellor
Chardonnay
Pinot Noir
Riesling
Vignoles

WINES PRODUCED:
Chardonnay
Cayuga White
Johannisberg Riesling (dry)
Johannisberg Riesling (semi-dry)
Trio–*a blend of Cayuga, Vignoles, and Chancellor*
Duet–*a blend of Cayuga and Vignoles*
Solo–*100% Vignoles*
Chancellor
Pinot Noir
Late Harvest Solo–*100% Vignoles*
Late Harvest Johannisberg Riesling

RECENT AWARDS:
1989 Cayuga White–*1991 New York Wine & Food Classic, Silver Medal*
1989 Chancellor–*1991 NYW&FC, Bronze Medal*
1990 Cayuga White–*1991 International Eastern Wine Competition, Silver Medal*
1990 Johannisberg Riesling (semi-dry)–*Intervin International, Bronze Medal*
1990 Chancellor–*San Diego National Wine Competition, Bronze Medal*

PRICING:
$5.00 to $11.50 per bottle; quantity discounts available.
MasterCard and Visa accepted.

AVAILABILITY: At restaurants and liquor stores throughout central New York.

TASTINGS AND TOURS:

Open early May through October, daily, noon to 5 PM.
Open November through early May, Saturday and Sunday, noon to 4 PM,
  and by appointment.
$2.00 charge for tastings, includes souvenir wine glass.
Guided walking tour offered in season, daily, at 2:30 PM.

KNAPP VINEYARDS

Doug and Suzie Knapp met in Panama while Doug was working for an electronics contractor. In 1971, Doug purchased an old Finger Lakes farm and began growing grapes. Four years later, Doug and Suzie moved from Panama to tend the vineyards. They soon realized that future business success depended on them becoming wine producers as well as grape growers.

Doug believes that wine is made in the vineyards; without good grapes, good wine can't be made. That belief led to a major planting in 1978 of classic vinifera grapes—Chardonnay and Riesling. By growing all of the grapes used in their wines, the Knapps are able to tend and harvest them to yield the best possible wines.

The Knapps intend to continue expanding and are most enthusiastic about the future of red vinifera wines on Cayuga Lake. As Doug is fond of pointing out, the growing season in the Finger Lakes is often longer than that of the Loire Valley

and Bordeaux, touted home of premium wines. With this view, they've expanded their original plantings of Cabernet Sauvignon, Pinot Noir, Cabernet Franc, and Merlot—all red vinifera grape varieties. The goal at Knapp is to focus on vinifera wines.

Doug continues to hone his winemaking skills. He has recently incorporated a champagne-making method practiced by the French in which whole grapes clusters are put directly into the press, bypassing the crusher-stemmer. The wine is thus unmarred by the undesirable elements normally extracted from the stems and yields a softer, cleaner, more elegant wine. The Knapps

are pleased with their recently released Brut Champagne produced in this manner.

The Knapps are known for their annual festivals, pairing Doug's wines and Suzie's fabulous cooking. They start in April with a winemaker's dinner and barrel tasting weekend. Their June anniversary celebration is different every year. July features their elaborate champagne brunch, and September's harvest festival features a pig roast and live music. Their fall winemaker's dinner and new wine party arrives in November, and December brings their Champagne Club holiday gala, an elegant event for Champagne Club members only.

1992 marked a major expansion in the Knapp family business tradition. Suzie's son, Jeffrey Adema and his wife Louise will open The Restaurant at Knapp Vineyards. Jeffrey, a graduate of the Culinary Institute of America is the chef. Louise, a native of Holland, brings five years of restaurant management experience to Knapp. Doug's daughter, Lori, joined her father as assistant winemaker in 1991.

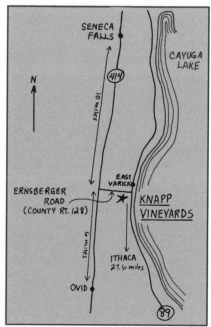

KNAPP VINEYARDS

Ernsberger Road, County Road 128, Romulus, NY 14541
Phone: (607) 869-9271

OWNERS: Doug and Suzie Knapp

WINEMAKER: Doug Knapp

ESTABLISHED:
Property purchased 1971
First planting 1972
First vintage 1982

PRODUCTION:
75 acres planted
60 acres in production
39,000 gallon capacity
Grapes are sold.

GRAPES GROWN:

Cabernet Franc	Pinot Noir
Cabernet Sauvignon	Riesling
Cayuga White	Seyval Blanc
Chardonnay	Vidal
Merlot	Vignoles

WINES PRODUCED:
Brut–*a sparkling wine made from Pinot Noir and Chardonnay*
Blanc de Blanc Champagne–*made from Vignoles*
Chardonnay
Riesling
Seyval
Seashore White–*made from Seyval and Chardonnay*
Dutchman's Breeches–*a blend of Vignoles and Vidal*
Vignoles
Lady's Slipper–*a blush wine made from Cayuga and Cabernet Sauvignon*
Pasta Red–*a blend including Baco Noir*
Cabernet Franc
Pinot Noir
Cabernet Sauvignon
Late Harvest Riesling
Late Harvest Vignoles
George's Peach–*made from peaches*

RECENT AWARDS: Consistently receive awards in national and international competitions.

PRICING:
$4.95 to $11.99 per bottle, with Chardonnay Champagne at $17.95; case discounts available.
MasterCard and Visa accepted.

AVAILABILITY: Throughout New York State and Massachusetts.

TASTINGS AND TOURS:

Open April through December, Monday through Saturday, 10 AM to 5 PM; Sunday, noon to 5 PM.
The Restaurant at Knapp Vineyards is open daily for lunch and Friday and Saturday for dinner.
$2.00 charge for tasting and souvenir wine glass.
Tour at 1 PM daily.

LAKESHORE WINERY

1990

GEWURZTRAMINER

Cayuga Lake Table Wine
CONTAINS SULFITES
Produced and Bottled by Lakeshore Winery
5132 Rt. 89, Romulus, N.Y. 14541

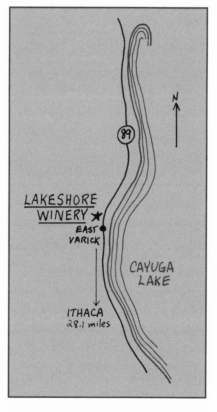

A small winery as warm and personal as its owner, Lakeshore Winery is housed in a nineteenth-century barn. Owner Bill Brown often personally conducts tastings in the stone-floored tasting area furnished with chairs and wooden settees. In the loft upstairs, his wife Doris displays antiques and crafts available for purchase.

A graduate of Cornell University, Bill worked as a Cooperative Extension agent for twenty-nine years and now asserts his knowledge and opinions at his own winery. Bill cultivates the low-yielding vinifera, including the difficult Cabernet Sauvignon grape, because he thinks they make superior wines. He uses special oak barrels, yielding a unique, rich taste in his oak-aged wines.

At three acres, Lakeshore is one of the smaller wineries in the region. However, Bill buys grapes and in a good growing year will make all the wine he can. He ages his wine generously and on occasion has released a ten-year-old vintage. His latest venture, *methode champenoise* sparkling Chardonnay, was well received, and Bill will continue making it in the future.

Virginia Lott, responsible for foods at the winery, offers tidbits of food with a chosen wine, demonstrating how each enhances the other. Always discovering new combinations, they welcome suggestions. Virginia orchestrates an annual dinner in November entitled "Babette's Feast," a ten-to-twelve-course dinner with matching wines. Seating, by invitation only, is quite limited.

Dedicated to the industry, Bill is strongly committed to the future, united growth of the area's wineries, to sharing technological advances, and to continuing his support for the cooperative promotion of the wine trails.

LAKESHORE WINERY

5132 Route 89, Romulus, NY 14541
Phone: (315) 549-8461

OWNERS:	Bill and Doris Brown
WINEMAKER:	Bill Brown
ESTABLISHED:	Property purchased 1977 First planting 1978 First vintage 1982
PRODUCTION:	3 acres planted 3 acres in production 4000 gallon yield Grapes are purchased.
GRAPES GROWN:	Cabernet Sauvignon Chardonnay Gewurztraminer Riesling
WINES PRODUCED:	Chardonnay–*a sparkling wine* Chardonnay Riesling Gewurztraminer Uncle Charlie–*a blend of Riesling, Chardonnay, Baco Noir, and Catawba* Aunt Clara–*a blend of Diamond, Dutchess, and Catawba* Chateau Côte du Lac–*made from Baco Noir* Cabernet Sauvignon
RECENT AWARDS:	Do not enter competitions.
PRICING:	$4.00 to $14.00 per bottle; discounts available. MasterCard and Visa accepted.
AVAILABILITY:	At the winery only.
TASTINGS AND TOURS:	Open May through November, Monday through Saturday, 11 AM to 5 PM; Sunday, noon to 5 PM. There may be a charge for tastings. Informal tour upon request.

SWEDISH HILL VINEYARD

The Petersons didn't intend to start a winery–Cindy was vice president of a bank, and Dick worked with the Seneca Falls school district. But after moving to this Seneca County farm, they were inspired by grape-growing friends to plant a few acres. By 1975 they had thirty acres planted; they opened their winery eleven years later. Its success prompted the Petersons to leave their full-time jobs in order to devote themselves entirely to the farm and winery.

Swedish Hill has earned an excellent reputation. They are able to sell most of their wine right at the winery even though they've increased production more than tenfold since opening. Cindy and Dick have already added onto their recently built tasting room and built a new warehouse just to keep up with their growth.

The cathedral-ceilinged cedar tasting area has two wooden tasting bars in the front room and one in the back. This back room has an array of equipment on sale for serious home winemakers, including crusher-stemmers, wine presses, tanks, filters, and barrels.

Swedish Hill offers gift packages, specialized labels for holidays, weddings, and other occasions, and they'll even print personalized labels. Using hybrid and vinifera grapes, the Petersons offer a wide variety of wines. Their most recent releases include a Port-style wine, Bordeaux-style red wine, and two sparkling wines.

The Petersons hold several annual events—they start with Cabin Fever Days in March, celebrate their anniversary in May, hold a Scandinavian Festival in June, a Wine & Art Festival in August, a Dessert Wine Festival in November, and honor Santa Lucia Day in December. Horse-drawn wagon rides through the vineyard are offered weekend afternoons, Memorial Day through October, weather permitting. Call ahead for details. Bus tours can be easily accommodated, and the knowledgeable staff adds to the friendly atmosphere.

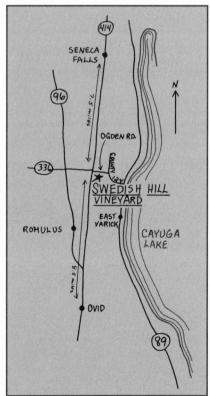

SWEDISH HILL VINEYARD

4565 Route 414, Romulus, NY 14541
Phone: (315) 549-8326

OWNERS: Dick and Cindy Peterson

WINEMAKER: Tim Miller

ESTABLISHED: Property purchased 1968
First planting 1969
First vintage 1985

PRODUCTION: 30 acres planted
30 acres in production
40,000 gallon yield
Some grapes are purchased.

GRAPES GROWN:

Aurore
Cabernet Franc
Cabernet Sauvignon
Catawba
Chardonnay
Merlot
Ventura
Vignoles

Champagne Brut–*100% Chardonnay*
Blanc de Blanc Champagne–*a hybrid blend of Chardonnay*
Champagne–*Spumante Blush*
Chardonnay
Private Reserve–*a blend of Chardonnay and Vignoles*
Chablis–*a changing blend, often including Aurore, Cayuga, Ventura, and Vignoles*
Dry Riesling
Johannisberg Riesling
Cayuga White
Vignoles
Ventura
Svenska White–*a blend of Catawba and Vignoles*
Svenska Blush–*a blend of Catawba, Ventura, Aurore, and Baco Noir*
Reserve Rosé–*a blend of Riesling, Vignoles, and Foch*
Svenska Red–*a blend of Aurore, Concord, Foch, and Ives*
Chancellor
Marechal Foch
Baco Noir
Vignoles Special Reserve
Vignoles Late Harvest
Cynthia Marie–*a Port-style dessert wine*

RECENT AWARDS:	Consistently receive numerous awards, including: 1991 Dry Riesling–*1992 Tasters Guild International, Silver Medal; 1992 International Eastern Wine Competition, Silver Medal* 1991 Johannisberg Riesling–*1992 San Diego National Wine Competition, Silver Medal* 1990 Johannisberg Riesling–*1991 TGI, Silver Medal; 1991 Atlanta Wine Summit International Competition, Silver Medal* 1990 Cayuga White–*1991 IEWC, Silver Medal; 1991 AWSIC, Silver Medal* 1990 Reserve Rosé–*1991 IEWC, Silver Medal; 1991 AWSIC, Silver Medal* 1990 Svenska White–*1991 AWSIC, Silver Medal* 1990 Chancellor–*1992 New World International Wine Competition, Gold Medal; 1992 TGI, Gold Medal; 1992 SDNWC, Silver Medal* 1990 Baco Noir–*1992 SDNWC, Silver Medal* 1990 Marechal Foch–*1991 AWSIC, Silver Medal* 1990 Svenska Red–*1991 IEWC, Gold Medal* 1990 Late Harvest Vignoles–*1992 TGI, Gold Medal; 1992 NWIWC, Silver Medal; 1991 Grand Harvest Awards (sponsored by Pierce's Restaurant, Elmira), Silver Medal*
PRICING:	$4.99 to $12.99 per bottle; case discounts available. MasterCard, Visa, and Discover Card accepted.
AVAILABILITY:	At restaurants and liquor stores in central and western New York.
TASTINGS AND TOURS: 	Open year round, Monday through Saturday, 9 AM to 6 PM; Sunday, noon to 6 PM. Closed Thanksgiving, Christmas, and New Year's Day. $1.00 charge for tastings, refunded with purchase. Guided tours available May through October, weekdays, 1 PM and 3 PM; weekends, noon, 2 PM, and 4 PM. Horse-drawn wagon rides through the vineyards offered Memorial Day through October, weekend afternoons, weather permitting.

KING FERRY WINERY

Peter and Tacie Saltonstall are long-time residents of King Ferry. When friends wanted to start a winery, the Saltonstalls offered to plant vineyards on their land. Although not previously involved in winemaking, they immersed themselves completely in the project, seeking advice from regional experts, visiting France, and doing every step themselves.

So when the Saltonstalls' friends had to back out of their plans, Peter and Tacie were left with a well-equipped winery, vineyards ready to yield wine, plenty of newly acquired knowledge, and a professional consultant to help them through. They opened in December 1989, offering two styles each of Chardonnay and Riesling. They employ three types of oak barrels, use all hand-picked grapes, and strive for smooth, clean, sophisticated wines.

The Saltonstalls now also produce limited quantities of Gewurztraminer and Pinot Noir and have added a new Riesling, Spätgold. For this wine, they leave the Riesling grapes on the vine an additional three weeks to produce a spätlese-style wine with the extra character and fruit overtones of late harvest wines, but not as sweet or syrupy.

This winery, the first in Cayuga County and the first ever on the east side of Cayuga Lake, is considered a part of the Cayuga Lake appellation. Most of the other Cayuga Lake wineries line the lake's western shore; the drive to King Ferry offers a different, westerly view of Cayuga Lake.

Since opening, the Saltonstalls have significantly increased the winery's facilities, with sufficient room for oak ageing. Tacie and a friend hand painted the new tasting room walls with colorful vineyard and winery scenes. The long tile-topped tasting bar can accommodate many visitors, and tastings can overflow into the barrel ageing area.

The Saltonstalls are pleased with their wines' style, and look forward to the ever-increasing character that will come as the vines continue maturing. They intend to limit production so they can maintain a high quality product, to continue hand picking all the grapes, and to remain personally involved in every step of their winery from pruning to labelling. Distribution is limited to selected local and Manhattan restaurants and liquor stores.

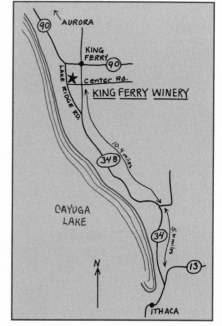

KING FERRY WINERY

658 Lake Road, King Ferry, NY 13081
Phone: (315) 364-5100

OWNERS: Peter and Tacie Saltonstall

WINEMAKER: Peter Saltonstall

ESTABLISHED: Property purchased 1948
First planting 1984
First vintage 1988

PRODUCTION: 17 acres planted

12 acres in production
3,500 gallon yield
Grapes are neither purchased nor sold.

GRAPES GROWN: Chardonnay

Gewurztraminer
Pinot Noir
Riesling

WINES PRODUCED: **Treleaven label:**
Chardonnay
Reserve Chardonnay
Dry Riesling
Semi-dry Riesling
Gewurztraminer
Spätgold–*made from Riesling*
Treleaven Saumon–*a blush wine blending Pinot Noir and Chardonnay*
Pinot Noir

RECENT AWARDS: 1989 Reserve Chardonnay–*1991 New York Wine & Food Classic, Silver Medal*
1989 Chardonnay–*1991 NYW&FC, Bronze Medal*
1989 Dry Riesling–*1991 International Eastern Wine Competition, Bronze Medal*
1988 Reserve Chardonnay–*1990 Atlanta Wine Competition, Silver Medal*
1988 Chardonnay–*1990 Intervin, Bronze Medal; 1991 NYW&FC, Bronze Medal*

PRICING: $7.99 to $15.99 per bottle; discounts available.
MasterCard and Visa accepted.

AVAILABILITY: At limited Ithaca, Rochester, Syracuse, and New York City restaurants and
liquor stores and the New York City Greenmarket.

TASTINGS AND TOURS: Open February through April, Saturday and Sunday, 1 PM to 5 PM.

Open May through December, daily, 1 PM to 5 PM.
$2.25 charge for tastings and souvenir wine glass.
Informal tour of winery and vineyards available.

SIGNORE WINERY

Donato Signore grew up helping his father make wine every year at their home in Chicago, and he didn't enjoy it one bit. Over the years, his attitude toward winemaking has changed. Now, calling upon the techniques he learned years ago, Donato has his own winery.

The Signores met in Alaska. While visiting Ann's family in Ithaca in the 1950's, they decided this would be a nice place to settle, and moved out to a secluded farm in Brooktondale.

Donato enjoys working. After retiring from Cornell University, he started working full-time as an architect and in 1981 started making wine. He decided to open this winery in 1989, unaware of the annoying burden of legally required paperwork.

In addition to all of the administrative work, another important task for Signore is marketing. Since he is off the beaten track of the wine trails, he must work to increase awareness of his wines and winery. However, Donato enjoys the winemaking process, and his proximity to Ithaca encourages increasing numbers of Cornellians to visit.

Although of proud Italian heritage, Donato's first trip to Italy was his recent working visit to a winery in Tuscany with his wife. He has refined his techniques through winemaking seminars at Cornell University. Buying all of his grapes, Donato concentrates on winemaking, tampering as little as possible with the grapes to achieve clean, crisp, sophisticated wines.

Tastings are offered in the cozy winery, at a table set up in front of the solo wine tank. Donato is planting an Italian garden where tastings may be offered in warm weather. A new tasting room is also in the planning stage. Donato intends to keep his winery quite small, selling only at the winery and Ithaca stores.

19 90
SIGNORE
Chardonnay
FINGER LAKES TABLE WINE
MADE & BOTTLED BY DANIEL M. SIGNORE, BROOKTONDALE, NY 14817
ALCOHOL 11% BY VOLUME   750ML.   CONTAINS SULFITES

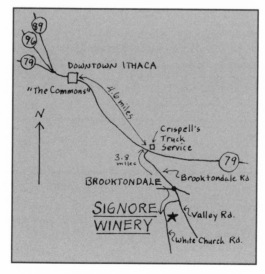

SIGNORE WINERY

153 White Church Road, Brooktondale, NY 14817
Phone: (607) 539-7935

OWNER: Donato (Dan) Signore

WINEMAKER: Donato Signore

ESTABLISHED: Property purchased 1959
First vintage 1989

PRODUCTION: 1000 gallon yield
All grapes are purchased

WINES PRODUCED: Chardonnay
Riesling
Classic White—*a blend of Cayuga and Vignoles*
Pinot Noir
Baco Noir

RECENT AWARDS: Do not enter competitions.

PRICING: $4.29 to $7.99 per bottle; case discounts available.
Credit cards are not accepted.

AVAILABILITY: At Ithaca liquor stores.

TASTINGS AND TOURS: Open April through December, Saturday and Sunday, noon to 5 PM,
and by appointment.
No charge for tastings.
Informal tour available.

SIX MILE CREEK VINEYARD

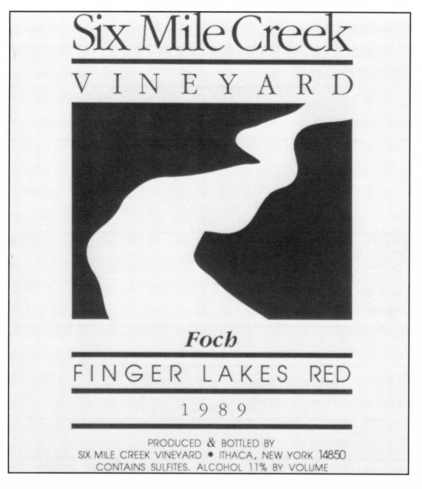

Six Mile Creek

V I N E Y A R D

Foch

FINGER LAKES RED

1989

PRODUCED & BOTTLED BY
SIX MILE CREEK VINEYARD • ITHACA, NEW YORK 14850
CONTAINS SULFITES. ALCOHOL 11% BY VOLUME

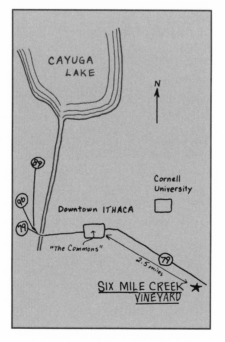

A professor of Health Policy and Management at Cornell University, Roger Battistella was a home wine-maker for years and an active participant in amateur competitions. When the twenty-four acres next door came up for sale, it was an opportunity he couldn't pass by. Roger and his family planted vines, moved the barn back off the road and onto a new foundation, and started winemaking in earnest. Painstakingly restored, one step at a time, the barn presently holds the tasting room and winemaking operation on the first floor. The vineyards behind the winery run into a wooded valley, and a pre-Civil War burial ground abuts the vineyard.

Roger and Nancy work at Six Mile Creek Winery while managing full-time commitments outside the operation. They intend to stay small, selling most of their wine from the premises and through local restaurants and retailers. Roger is pleased that as his vineyard matures it is yielding ever-higher quality wines. He's made modest improvements in the sales area and in winemaking equipment, and envisions selling 2000 cases annually at the winery.

October brings their annual Anniversary Harvest Festival. Visitors taste newly released wines, sample hors d'oeuvres, and enjoy live music. The Battistellas are currently planning a Wine and Herb Sensation, matching wines and various select herbed foods. Call for details.

Located only two miles from Ithaca, this was the first winery in Tompkins County. The winery and some of the blended wines bear local names; Six Mile Creek is nearby, and Cascadilla White celebrates neighboring Cascadilla Creek.

SIX MILE CREEK VINEYARD

1551 Slaterville Road, Route 79, Ithaca, NY 14850
Phone: (607) 273-6219

OWNERS: Roger M. and Nancy S. Battistella

WINEMAKER: Roger M. Battistella

ESTABLISHED:
Property purchased 1981
First planting 1982
First vintage 1987

PRODUCTION:

6 acres planted
6 acres in production
3,400 gallon yield
Red grapes are purchased.

GRAPES GROWN:

Cayuga
Chardonnay
Riesling
Seyval
Vidal
Vignoles

WINES PRODUCED:

Chardonnay
Riesling
Seyval
Cayuga White
Ravat Vignoles
Ithaca White—*a blend of Vidal, Vignoles, Riesling, and Chardonnay*
Cascadilla White—*a blend of Vignoles and Cayuga*
Pasa Tiempo—*a blend of Seyval, Vidal, and Aurore*
Odyssey Blush—*a blend of Seyval, Vidal, and DeChaunac*
Foch
DeChaunac
Baco Noir
Chancellor
Ithaca Red—*a blend of DeChaunac, Baco Noir, and Foch*

RECENT AWARDS: Have not entered competitions recently.

PRICING:
$5.50 to $10.00 per bottle; case discounts available.
MasterCard and Visa accepted.

AVAILABILITY: Available at selected local restaurants and liquor stores.

TASTINGS AND TOURS:

Open June through December, daily, noon to 5:30 PM.
Open January through May, Saturday and Sunday, noon to 5:30 PM,
  and by appointment.
$1.00 charge for tastings, refunded with purchase.
Informal tours are available.

MAJOR WINE VARIETIES AVAILABLE BY WINERY

○ included in a blended wine

	Sparkling Wine	Chardonnay	Riesling	Gewürztraminer	Russian Grapes	Seyval	Vignoles	Cayuga	Niagara	Catawba	Blush Wine	Hybrid Red Wine	Pinot Noir	Merlot	Cabernet Sauvignon	Late Harvest Wine	Sherry/Port
Amberg Wine Cellars		●	●								●		●				
Americana Vineyards			●			●		●	○	●	●				●		
Anthony Road Wine Company		●	●			●	●						●		●		
Arbor Hill Grapery	●	●	●	○			●	○		●	●	●			●		
Barrington Champagne Company	●																
Bully Hill Vineyards	●					●	●	●			●	●			●		
Cana Vineyards Winery	●	●	●		○		●	○			●	●					
Canandaigua Wine Company	●	●	●			●				●	●	●			●		●
Casa Larga Vineyards	●	●	●	●		●					●	●			●		
Castel Grisch Estate Winery	●	●	●			●				●	●	●			●		
Cayuga Ridge Estate Vineyard		●	●				●				●	●	●		●		
Chateau LaFayette Reneau		●	●			●			●	○	●	○	●		●		
Dr. Frank's Vinifera Wine Cellars	●	●	●	●	●						●	●			●	●	
Eagle Crest Vineyards					○	○	○		●		●						●
Four Chimneys Farm Winery	●	●				●					●	●			●		
Fox Run Vineyards	●	●	●								●				●		
Frontenac Point Vineyard		●	●			●					●	●	○		●		
Fulkerson Wine Cellars		●	●			●	●				●	●			●		
Giasi Winery		●	●			●	●				●	●		●			
Glenora Wine Cellars	●	●	●			●	●				●			●			
Hazlitt 1852 Vineyards		●	●			●	●		●		●	●			●		
Heron Hill Vineyards		●	●			●	○	●			●	●			●		
Hosmer		●	●			●	●				●		●				
Hunt Country Vineyards		●	●			●	●				●	●			●		
Keuka Spring Vineyards		●	●			●	●	○			●						
King Ferry Winery		●	●	●							●		●				
Knapp Vineyards	●	●	●			●	●	○			●	●			●		
Lakeshore Winery	●	●	●						○		●		●				
Lakewood Vineyards		●	●				●	●	●	●	●	●			●		
Lamoreaux Landing Wine Cellars	●	●	●								●		●	●	○	●	
Lucas Vineyards	●	●	●			●	○	○			●	●			●		
McGregor Vineyard Winery	●	●	●	●	●	●	●				●	●			●		
New Land Vineyard		●	●								●		●				
Poplar Ridge Vineyards	●				○		●		●	●	●	●			○		
Prejean Winery		●	●			●					●	●		●	●		
Rolling Vineyards		●	●			●		●			●				●		
Signore Winery		●	●			○	○				●		●				
Six Mile Creek Vineyard		●	●			●	●				●		●				
Squaw Point Winery	●	●	●			●		●	○		●			○	●		
Swedish Hill Vineyard	●	●	●				●		○		●			○	○		●
Taylor–Great Western–Gold Seal	●	●	●			●	●		●		●		●		●		●
Thorpe Vineyard		●	○				●						●				
Wagner Vineyards		●	●			●	●	○			●	●			●		
Widmer's Wine Cellars	●	●	●			●		○			●	●			●		
Hermann J. Wiemer Vineyard	●	●	●	○									●		●		

116

GRAPE VARIETIES

Vinifera (European)

White

Chardonnay
Gewurztraminer
Johannisberg Riesling
Muscat Ottonel
Pinot Gris
Rkatsiteli
Saperavi
Sauvignon Blanc
Sereksia

Red

Cabernet Sauvignon
Carmine
Merlot
Pinot Meunier
Pinot Noir

French-American Hybrids

White

Aurore
Cayuga White
L'Ambertille
Rayon d'Or
Seyval Blanc
Verdelet
Vidal
Vignoles (Ravat 51)
Villard Blanc

Red

Baco Noir
Chambourcin
Chancellor
Chelois
DeChaunac
Leon Millot
Marechal Foch
Rougeon
Villard Noir
Vincent

Labrusca (Native American)

White

Catawba
Delaware
Diamond
Dutchess
Elvira
Isabella
Niagara

Red

Concord
Ives
Steuben

WINERY INDEX